WEBER

WOOD PELLET GRILL

COOKBOOK

1000-DAY GRILL RECIPES FOR REAL BARBECUE TO GRILL MEAT

FRED DILLARD

CONTENTS

INTRODUCTION

What IS Weber Wood Pellet Grill?

Wood Pellet grills utilize ignited wood pellets and a system of fans to heat food to a specific temperature, quite like an outdoor convection oven. Pellet grills can be used to smoke, grill, bake and even braise food. Nearly anything you make in a standard oven can be made on a pellet grill.

How does Weber Wood Pellet Grill work?

The heat is generated from wood pellets that are placed in a chamber called a "pellet hopper." Those pellets move through an auger to a fire pot, which heats the entire cooking chamber of the grill. Through a fan system, heat and smoke are dispensed throughout the grill, providing a naturally rich and woody flavor from the pellets. Though pellet grills certainly share some characteristics of your traditional grills, there are a couple of major differences that set pellet grills apart: most notably, the combination of deep flavor, versatility and efficiency.

Why People Choose the Weber Wood Pellet Grill?

1.Weber WOOD PELLET GRILL IS EASY TO USE

One of the greatest features of a pellet grill is the fact they're easy to use. Simply fill the hopper with food-grade wood pellets, empty the ash pail, and select your desired temperature and smoke level. The pellet grill takes over from there as an electric auger feeds the burn pot with wood pellets from the hopper.

Once you set the temperature, the pellet grill maintains it and feeds wood pellets as needed. Pellet grills are highly precise with temperature control from their lowest to highest settings (180-500 degrees on many grills).

For even more accurate control, grill blankets are available to help pellet grills hold in more heat and smoke. They maintain even more consistent temperatures throughout the entire year, but they're especially useful in the winter months when outside temperatures drop.

Pellet grills are also easy to clean when you're finished cooking. Whether it's a quick clean-up or a deeper clean, no effort takes longer than 15 minutes to maintain your grill.

2. SET IT & FORGET IT

With pellet grills, you can set it and walk away. Since the grill does all the work, you get a wood-fired taste without having to constantly feed logs or wood chunks. Overall, pellet grills do not require as much time or attention, and there's no need to constantly check the grill temperature or level of smoke.

Newer models even monitor temperature levels from the palm of your hand. Traeger and Camp Chef now both feature, easy-to-use, WiFi controlling technology. Change the temperature, adjust smoke levels, and receive notifications from your phone.

3. VERSATILITY TO COOK ANYTHING

Naturally, a pellet grill is great for smoking and grilling, but it's also the centerpiece for much more. All of your favorite dishes that are usually cooked inside can now be done outdoors. Think of it as a kitchen in your backyard where you can perfectly cook anything with confidence.

➢ BBQ

Traditional smokers have set the BBQ bar for a long time and are debated to provide a better smoke. On the opposite side of that argument are pellet grills. Pellet grills are now recognized for their quality and are even sanctioned in contests sponsored by the Kansas City Barbeque Society (KCBS), winning many bbq competitions in recent years.

The combination of smoke quality and convenience with pellet grills is unbeatable. Taste all of your barbecue favorites from the comfort of your own backyard. Pick your favorite wood pellet flavors, set the grill on low and go. You'll love the beautiful smoke ring, tenderness, and delicious flavor you get from home cooked ribs, pulled pork, beef brisket, chicken quarters and wings. Fresh salmon, trout, and even sides such as mac and cheese are wonderfully smoky and tasty.

➢ BAKE

Anything cooked in an oven can be done in a pellet grill. Pellet grills primarily work as a convection oven. Indirect heat and smoke are produced from the burn pot and blown around the pellet grill for a perfect, evenly cooked finish. Bake breads, cakes, pies, breakfast casseroles, and delicious, wood-fired pizzas. Plus, when you bake your favorites outside in the summer months, you avoid heating up your house and kitchen.

➢ GRILL

For many of our common grilling favorites–such as summer burgers and hot dogs–there's a time when we need to turn up the heat. Pork chops and your favorite cuts of steak or chicken are fabulous when cooked over a wood fire. Don't forget your vegetables too!

Pellet grills used to only have an indirect heat option, but that has changed in recent years. To improve the grilling feature, many manufacturers now offer models with perforated drip trays, direct heat over the burn pot, and/or temperatures up to 500°. This allows your burgers and steaks to sizzle and get those beautiful grill marks and a good crust on the outside, while still preserving a medium to rare center.

4. GREAT WOOD-FIRED FLAVORS

While there are many grilling options out there, nothing produces better tasting food than a pellet grill. Fuel flavors your food and with wood-fired flavors are superior to gas and charcoal alternatives. All of your favorite dishes are simply better on a pellet grill.

With pellet grills, you also have flavor options when choosing wood pellets for your grill. Each pellet flavor, or type of wood, has a unique taste that naturally complements and enhances your favorite foods. Specific hardwood blends are also available. Experiment with different food-grade wood pellet options and find the flavors you and your family enjoy the most.

How to Use the Weber Wood Pellet Grill?

For wood pellet newcomers, pellet grills and smokers are an excellent way to get into barbecue. Learn how to get the best out of your wood cooker with our step-by-step guide to using a pellet smoker grill.

1. Season your pellet smoker.

Before we do anything, we need to season the smoker. This is a crucial step for any type of new smoker, and helps protect it from the negative effects of long term continuous use. The basic premise is to apply cooking oil to the grates and inside of the chamber and then take the smoker on a 'dry run' without food. This will cook the oil onto the inside surfaces of the smoker, forming a protective layer across it. After you have seasoned it, leave the smoker to cool and rest for at least 24 hours before using properly.

2. Preheat your smoker.

A big pain with charcoal grills is heating them up. Lighting them and keeping them at a good temperature can be tricky. Not so with a pellet grill. They work much in the same way as an oven.

With your grill plugged in to an electric outlet or socket, switch it on and select your target temperature. If you're going for barbecue smoking, choose 225°F (107°C).

Most smokers will take about 10 minutes to preheat and come to temperature.

You should hear a dull roar come from the smoker as it heats up. This is the motorized auger and firebox springing into action, and is a good sign that your smoker is working and warming up.

Pro tip: While pellet smokers do have a temperature gauge on their control display, it's not unusual for these to be inaccurate by up to about 20°F either way. Get a dual probe smoker thermometer. These allow you to simultaneously measure cooking and internal meat temperatures. The best models are more accurate than the majority of built-in gauges.

3. Add your meat.

With your pellet smoker now running at target temperature, carefully place your meat on the smoker grates. For the best results, place the food in the middle of the grate. This will ensure that the meat is far away enough from the heat to not dry out, but close enough to be cooked at temperature.

4. Pay attention to fat content.

A mistake that a lot of BBQ newcomers make is with the meat itself. Meat that is too lean can dry out quickly, whereas meat with too much fat content can get in the way of the smoke working its way into the flesh of the meat.

If you choose to smoke a cut like brisket, then be sure that you trim the layer of fat on it to about ½ inch thick before putting it on the smoker.

How to Clean and Care for Your Weber Wood Pellet Grill?

> ➢ **BETWEEN EACH COOK**

For quick cleanup between cookouts, you don't need to do anything too dramatic. In fact, our patented Ash Cleanout system makes it as simple as pulling a knob. Before you fire up the grill each time, just empty the ash into the cup, and you're good to go. It's almost too easy.

Don't forget about the internal temperature probe. You'll want to clean it between each cook. It's located on the right side of the cooking chamber and is about the size of a pencil. Our goal is to keep it looking silver. To do this mixt a vinegar/water solution and use a scouring pad. Often times if your temperature does not read accurately it's because too much smoke has been build up.

Besides emptying the burn cup, you may want to spot clean between cook sessions as well. This can be as simple as wiping away grease spots or food residue on the lid or side shelf. You should also scrape down the grill grates with a wire grill brush or spatula before you start cooking to avoid a burnt taste on your food.

If you take these small steps toward keeping your pellet grill clean, any deeper cleaning you do will be much easier.

> ➢ **EXTERIOR**

Safety first! Make sure your grill is totally cool, then unplug it from its power source.

Empty the pellet hopper to prevent your pellets from getting wet or coming into contact with cleaning substances.

Spray stainless steel cleaner on the painted or stainless steel surfaces of your grill. Avoid spraying any plastic components. (You can also use hot, soapy water-it just may not work as quickly!)

Let the cleaner sit for about 30 seconds to give it a chance to break down grease and smoke stains.

Wipe off the cleaner with a clean paper towel or rag. Wipe with the grain if you're cleaning stainless steel or in circles, if you're cleaning a painted surface.

Repeat the process once more to clean off any remaining grease or smoke. With a rag, rinse thoroughly if you used soapy water.

Allow to dry for at least 24 hours before cooking, and double-check that the hopper has no water in it before reloading pellets.

> **INTERIOR**

Pull the Ash Cleanout knob and empty the ash from the burn cup.

Open the lid and remove the cooking grate, any extra racks, drip tray, and heat diffuser plate from inside the grill. Pay attention to how these pieces are installed (or even take a picture) so you'll have an easier time reassembling your grill.

Use a wet/dry vacuum with a hose attachment to remove loose ash and debris.

Look for places inside your grill where grease has built up. Use something with a flat edge (a paint stick, pan scraper, etc.) to dislodge and remove it.

Use hot, soapy water and a rag you aren't attached to wash the interior of your grill, as well as each piece you pulled out.

Repeat the process until most of the grease buildup is gone.

With a rag, rinse thoroughly if you used soapy water and allow everything to dry.

Cover the heat diffuser plate and drip tray with aluminum foil for easier cleaning next time (you can simply throw away and replace the foil rather than scrubbing off the grease).

Allow to dry for at least 24 hours before cooking, and double-check that the hopper has no water in it before reloading pellets.

BAKING RECIPES

Baked Pumpkin Pie

Servings: 6

Cooking Time: 50 Minutes

Ingredients:

- 4 Ounce cream cheese
- 15 Ounce pumpkin puree
- 1/3 Cup Cream, whipping
- 1/2 Cup brown sugar
- 1 Teaspoon pumpkin pie spice
- 3 Large eggs
- 1 frozen pie crust, thawed

Directions:

1. Supply your smoker with wood pellets and follow the start-up procedure. Preheat the grill, with the lid closed, to 325° F.

2. Mix cream cheese, puree, milk, sugar, and spice. One at a time, incorporate an egg to the mixture. Pour mixture into pie shell.

3. Bake for 50 minutes, edges should be golden and pie should be firm around edges with slight movement in middle. Let cool before whip cream is applied. Serve and enjoy! Grill: 325 °F

Basil Margherita Pizza

Servings: 6

Cooking Time: 25 Minutes

Ingredients:

- Basil, Chopped
- 2 Cups Flour, All-Purpose
- Mozzarella Cheese, Sliced Rounds
- 1 Cup Pizza Sauce
- 1 Teaspoon Salt
- 1 Teaspoon Sugar
- 1 Tomato, Sliced
- 1 Cup Water, Warm
- 1 Teaspoon Yeast, Instant

Directions:

1. Combine the water, yeast, and sugar in a small bowl and let sit for about 5 minutes.

2. In a large bowl, stir together the flour and salt. Pour in the yeast mixture and mix until a soft dough forms. Knead for about 2 minutes. Place in an oiled bowl and cover with a cloth. Let the dough sit and rise for about 45 minutes or until the dough has doubled in size.

3. Roll out on a flat, floured surface (or on a pizza stone) until you''ve reached your desired shape and thickness.

4. Supply your smoker with wood pellets and follow the start-up procedure. Preheat the grill, with the lid closed, to 350° F.

5. On the rolled out dough, pour on the pizza sauce, cheese, and then tomatoes and basil. Place in your Grill and bake for about 25 minutes, or until the cheese is melted and slightly golden brown.

Sweet And Spicy Baked Pork Beans

Servings: 20

Cooking Time: 120 Minutes

Ingredients:

- 1 - 21 Oz Apple Pie Filling, Can
- 1 Gallon Baked Beans
- 1 Tbs Chilli, Powder
- 1 Green Bell Pepper, Diced
- 1 10 Oz Drained Jalapeno, Can Diced
- 1 Cup Maple Syrup
- 1 Onion, Diced
- 1 Lb Pork, Pulled

Directions:

1. Supply your smoker with wood pellets and follow the start-up procedure. Preheat the grill, with the lid closed, to 350° F.
2. Place all ingredients in mixing bowl and mix well.
3. Pour bean mixture into foil pans.
4. Bake in grill till bubbling throughout – about 2 hours.
5. Rest at least 15 minutes before serving.

Dark Chocolate Brownies With Bacon-salted Caramel

Servings: 8

Cooking Time: 40 Minutes

Ingredients:

- 8 Strips bacon
- 1/2 Cup kosher salt
- 1 Whole Brownie Mix
- 1 Jar caramel sauce

Directions:

1. For the bacon salt: Cook a few strips of bacon (6 to 8) until very crisp: 350 degrees for about 25 minutes should do it. Let cool, then pulse in a food processor until finely chopped. Mix with 1/2 cup kosher salt. Store in the refrigerator until ready to use.

2. Supply your smoker with wood pellets and follow the start-up procedure. Preheat the grill, with the lid closed, to 350° F.

3. Mix the brownies according to package directions and pour into a greased pan. Drizzle approximately 2 tablespoons of the caramel sauce over the brownie batter. Sprinkle with approximately 1 teaspoon of the bacon salt. Place directly on the grill grate of your preheated Traeger.

4. Bake the brownies for 20-25 minutes, until the batter has started to set up. Remove from the grill and drizzle with 2 more tablespoons of caramel sauce and sprinkle with more bacon salt. Return to the grill for 20-25 more minutes, or until a toothpick inserted in the middle of the brownies comes out clean.

5. If you like extra caramel, drizzle another layer of caramel on the hot brownies and sprinkle with a final bit of bacon salt. Allow the brownies to cool completely before cutting them into squares. Clean your knife in between each slice to prevent the brownies from sticking to the knife. Enjoy!

Italian Herb & Parmesan Scones

Servings: 8

Cooking Time: 20 Minutes

Ingredients:

- 2 1/2 Cup all-purpose flour
- 2 Teaspoon baking powder
- 1 Teaspoon baking soda
- 1/2 Teaspoon garlic salt
- 1 Tablespoon Italian Seasoning
- 1 Cup Parmesan cheese, grated
- 2 Large eggs
- 1 1/2 Cup buttermilk
- 1/4 Cup olive oil

Directions:

1. In a large mixing bowl, combine flour, baking powder, baking powder, soda, garlic salt, Italian seasoning, and 1/2 cup of the cheese. Make a well in the center.

2. In a smaller bowl, whisk together eggs, buttermilk, and olive oil.

3. Pour into the well in the dry ingredients, and stir batter just until it's combined. It will appear lumpy.

4. Oil 12 muffin cups, spray with cooking spray, or line with disposable paper liners.

5. Divide the batter evenly between the cups. Sprinkle the tops of the muffins with the remaining Parmesan cheese.

6. Supply your smoker with wood pellets and follow the start-up procedure. Preheat the grill, with the lid closed, to 400° F.

7. Arrange the muffin tin directly on the grill grate and bake the muffins for 20 to 25 minutes, or until a toothpick inserted in the center of the muffin comes out clean.

8. Cool for several minutes before removing from the muffin tin. Serve warm with butter or olive oil. Enjoy!

Vanilla Chocolate Bacon Cupcakes

Servings: 12

Cooking Time: 120 Minutes

Ingredients:

- 1 Lb Bacon
- 1 1/2 Tsp Baking Powder
- 1 1/2 Tsp Baking Soda
- 1 Cup Cocoa, Powder
- 2 Egg
- 1 3/4 Cups Flour
- 1 Cup Milk, Whole
- 1/2 Cup Oil
- 1 Tsp Salt
- 2 Cups Sugar
- 2 Tsp Vanilla

Directions:

1. Supply your smoker with wood pellets and follow the start-up procedure. Preheat the grill, with the lid closed, to 250° F.

2. Once your grill is preheated, place bacon strips on the grates. Smoke for 1hr-1 ½ hours or until desired crispiness is achieved.

3. Remove the bacon from the grill and set aside.

4. Increase set the temperature to 350°F and preheat.

5. Mix the rest of the ingredients in a bowl with an electric mixer until it is nice and smooth.

6. Pour the mixture into a cupcake tin.

7. Transfer the tin to your grill and bake for about 20 - 25 minutes.

8. Allow the cupcakes to cool on a wire rack. Once cooled, top with your favorite premade icing and a half of strip of the bacon. Serve and enjoy!

Easy Smoked Cornbread

Servings: 4

Cooking Time: 75 Minutes

Ingredients:

- 2 cups self rising flour
- 1 1/2 cups white corn meal
- 2 cups sharp cheddar cheese
- 1/2 cup sour cream
- 1/2 cup sugar
- 1 Tbsp baking powder
- 1 teaspoon sea salt
- 1 12 oz can of evaporated milk
- 1/2 cup vegetable oil
- 2 large eggs beaten

Directions:

1. Mix all ingredients together well and fold into a greased baking pan (such as a round cake Pan).

2. Supply your smoker with wood pellets and follow the start-up procedure. Preheat the grill, with the lid closed, to 375° F. Smoke on 375 °F for 1 hour and 15 minutes or until toothpick comes clean and edges look brown.

3. Rub some butter on top and sprinkle a little Fred's Butt Rub on top before serving.

4. Enjoy!

Blueberry Pancakes

Servings: 4

Cooking Time: 10 Minutes

Ingredients:

- ➢ 2 Cups Blueberries, Fresh
- ➢ 1 Cup Pancake Mix
- ➢ 1/2 Cup Sugar
- ➢ 3/4 Cup Water, Warm

Directions:

1. Supply your smoker with wood pellets and follow the start-up procedure. Preheat the grill, with the lid closed, to 350° F.

2. Place the cast iron griddle on the grates of your grill.

3. In a large bowl, pour water, pancake mix and 1/2 cup of the blueberries and mix until combined.

4. Pour the batter onto the griddle in 4 equal parts. Cook with the lid closed for about 6 minutes, or until the edges of the pancakes are slightly cooked. Flip each pancake and continue cooking for another 4 minutes.

5. Pour the hot blueberry sauce over your freshly cooked pancakes and enjoy!

Savory Cheesecake With Bourbon Pecan Topping

Servings: 6   Cooking Time: 75 Minutes

Ingredients:

- Crust
- 12 ounce Oreos
- 6 ounce melted butter
- Filling
- 24 ounces cream cheese - room temperature
- 1 cup granulated sugar
- 3 tbs cornstarch
- 2 large eggs
- 2/3 cup heavy cream
- 1 tbs vanilla
- 1 1/2 tbs bourbon

- Topping
- 3 large eggs beaten
- 1/3 cup granulated sugar
- 1/3 cup brown sugar
- 8 tbsp corn syrup dark corn syrup recommended
- 2 tbsp bourbon
- 1/2 tbsp vanilla
- 1/8 tbsp salt
- 3/4 cup rough chopped pecans (smoked pecans recommended)

Directions:

1. Supply your smoker with wood pellets and follow the start-up procedure. Preheat the grill, with the lid closed, to 350 °F.

2. Wrap foil on the bottom and up the sides of a 9" spring-form pan (outside of pan).

3. Butter the bottom & insides of the pan.

4. Crust

5. Throw ingredients in a food processor until they are finely ground.

6. Spread in 9" cheesecake pan on bottom & about ½ way upsides.

7. Filling

8. Place 8 oz of cream cheese in mixer bowl with 1/3 of sugar & cornstarch.Mix until smooth andcreamy.

9. Add another 8 oz cream cheese andbeat until smooth, then add remaining cream cheese,beating until smooth.

10. Then mix in the rest of the sugar, bourbon & vanilla.

11. Add eggs one at a time beating well after each one.

12. Add the heavy cream and mix just until smooth. Reminder: Do not over mix.

13. Pour batter into the prepared crust.

14. Topping

15. Mix all together except pecans.

16. Sprinkle pecans on top of cheesecake batter.

17. Pour topping over cheesecake batter.

18. Place in a pan big enough to hold a spring-form pan. Pour boiling water in the roasting pan to come up about ½ way up the spring-form pan.

19. Bake at 350 °F for 75 minutes until the top just barely jiggles. Carefully take the pan out of water-bath and put on cooling rack.

20. Let cool for 2 hours in pan. After 2 hours put in fridge until totally chilled then serve.

Grilled Beer Cheese Dip

Servings: 6

Cooking Time: 20 Minutes

Ingredients:

- ➢ 6 Oz Beer, Can
- ➢ 8 Oz Cream Cheese
- ➢ 1 Tsp Onion Powder
- ➢ ½ Tsp Pepper
- ➢ ½ Tsp Salt
- ➢ 2 Cups Shredded Cheese

Directions:

1. Supply your smoker with wood pellets and follow the start-up procedure. Preheat the grill, with the lid closed, to 350° F. If you're using a gas or charcoal grill, set it up for medium high heat. Preheat with lid closed for 10-15 minutes.

2. In the cast iron pan add cream cheese, shredded cheese, beer, onion powder, salt and pepper. Once grill is at 350°F place cast iron skillet onto the grill and cook for about 10 minutes, stir and cook for another 5-10 minutes.

3. Top with more shredded cheese and fresh parsley. Serve with fresh baked pretzels as well.

Rosemary Cranberry Apple Sage Stuffing

Servings: 7   Cooking Time: 45 Minutes

Ingredients:

- 10 Cups Day Old Diced Bread, Sliced Loaf
- 2 1/2 Cups Broth, Chicken
- 1 Cup Butter, Unsalted
- 1 Cup Diced Celery, Cut
- 1 1/2 Cups Fresh Cranberries
- 1 Beaten Egg
- 1 Medium Granny Smith Apple, Peel, Core And Dice
- 2 Tbsp Minced Parsley, Fresh
- 1 Tbsp Minced Rosemary, Fresh
- 2 Tbsp Roughly Chopped Sage
- Salt And Pepper
- 1 Tbsp Minced Thyme
- 2 Cups Diced Yellow Onion, Sliced

Directions:

1. Supply your smoker with wood pellets and follow the start-up procedure. Preheat the grill, with the lid closed, to 350° F.

2. Melt butter over medium heat. Add onions then celery and cook until onions start to become translucent.

3. In a large bowl, mix together bread, apples, cranberries, cooked onion and celery mixture, and fresh herbs.

4. Add half of the chicken broth to the mixture and stir.

5. Beat together eggs and the rest of the chicken broth in a small bowl. Pour into the bread mixture and stir until completely combined.

6. Add salt and pepper to taste.

7. Pour stuffing into a cast iron pan or baking dish. Cover with foil and bake on the grill for 30 minutes. Remove the foil and cook for an additional 15 minutes.

8. Serve immediately and enjoy!

SEAFOOD RECIPES

Baked Tuna Noodle Casserole

Servings: 4

Cooking Time: 45 Minutes

Ingredients:

- 1 Whole Wheat Pasta, Box (13.25oz)
- 2 Cup Yogurt
- 1 Cup almond milk
- 1 Teaspoon ground mustard
- 1/2 Teaspoon celery salt
- 1 Cup Button Mushrooms, Sliced
- 10 Ounce Tuna, Cooked
- 1 Cup Peas, canned
- 1 Cup Cheese, Colby/Cheddar

Directions:

1. Bring a large pot of salted water to a boil over high heat. Add pasta and cook according to manufacturer's directions. Drain and set aside.

2. In a medium bowl mix yogurt, milk, ground mustard, and celery salt. Fold in mushrooms, tuna, peas and cooked pasta. Fold in half the cheese.

3. Transfer the mixture to a greased 13" x 9" baking dish and top with remaining cheese.

4. Supply your smoker with wood pellets and follow the start-up procedure. Preheat the grill, with the lid closed, to 350° F.

5. Place casserole dish directly on grill grate and cook for 45 minutes or until warmed through and cheese is melted. Enjoy! Grill: 350 °F

Sweet Mandarin Salmon

Servings: 2

Cooking Time: 10 Minutes

Ingredients:

- 1 Whole lime juice
- 1 Teaspoon sesame oil
- 1 1/2 Cup Mandarin Orange Sauce
- 1 1/2 Tablespoon soy sauce
- 2 Tablespoon cilantro, finely chopped
- Freshly cracked black pepper
- 1 Whole (4 oz) wild salmon fillets

Directions:

1. Supply your smoker with wood pellets and follow the start-up procedure. Preheat the grill, with the lid closed, to 375° F.

2. For the glaze, combine Mandarin orange sauce, lime juice, sesame oil, soy sauce, cilantro and fresh cracked black pepper. Mix together.

3. Cut the salmon into 4 fillets. Brush with glaze and place directly on the grill grate, skin side down.

4. Cook until salmon reaches an internal temperature of 155 degrees F (about 15-20 minutes). Half way through cook time, brush salmon again with the glaze.

5. Remove the salmon from the grill and serve with remaining glaze if desired. Enjoy!

Mango Rice Wine Thai Shrimp

Servings: 4

Cooking Time: 15 Minutes

Ingredients:

- ➢ 2 Tablespoons Brown Sugar
- ➢ 2 Tablespoons Mango Magic Seasoning
- ➢ 1 Pinch (Optional) Red Pepper Flakes
- ➢ 1/2 Tablespoons Rice Wine Vinegar
- ➢ 1 Pound Raw Tail-On, Thaw And Deveined Shrimp, Uncooked
- ➢ 2 Tablespoons Soy Sauce
- ➢ 1 Teaspoon Sriracha Hot Sauce
- ➢ 1/2 Cup Sweet Chili Sauce

Directions:

1. Supply your smoker with wood pellets and follow the start-up procedure. Preheat the grill, with the lid closed, to 425° F. Rinse shrimp off in sink with cold water. Place in bowl and put in all of the ingredients listed above. Let marinade for 2 - 4 hours.

2. Thread several shrimp onto a skewer, so that they are all just touching each other. Repeat with other skewers and remaining shrimp.

3. Grill shrimp for 2 - 3 minutes on each side, or until pink and opaque all the way through. Remove from grill and serve immediately.

Garlic Blackened Catfish

Servings: 4

Cooking Time: 10 Minutes

Ingredients:

- ½ Cup Cajun Seasoning
- ¼ Tsp Cayenne Pepper
- 1 Tsp Granulated Garlic
- 1 Tsp Ground Thyme
- 1 Tsp Onion Powder
- 1 Tsp Ground Oregano
- 1 Tsp Pepper
- 4 (5-Oz.) Skinless Catfish Fillets
- 1 Tbsp Smoked Paprika
- 1 Stick Unsalted Butter

Directions:

1. In a small bowl, combine the Cajun seasoning, smoked paprika, onion powder, granulated garlic, ground oregano, ground thyme, pepper and cayenne pepper.

2. Sprinkle fish with salt and let rest for 20 minutes.

3. Supply your smoker with wood pellets and follow the start-up procedure. Preheat the grill, with the lid closed, to 450° F. If you're using a gas or charcoal grill, set it up for medium-high heat. Place cast iron skillet on the grill and let it preheat.

4. While grill is preheating, sprinkle catfish fillets with seasoning mixture, pressing gently to adhere. Add half the butter to preheated cast iron skillet and swirl to coat, add more butter if needed. Place fillets in hot skillet and cook 3-5 minutes or until a dark crust has been formed. Flip and cook an additional 3-5 minutes or until the fish flakes apart when pressed gently with your finger.

5. Remove fish from grill and sprinkle evenly with fresh parsley. Serve with lemon wedges and enjoy!

Smoked Fish Chowder

Servings: 4

Cooking Time: 60 Minutes

Ingredients:

- 12 Ounce (1-1/2 to 2 lb) skin-on salmon fillet, preferably wild-caught
- Fin & Feather Rub
- 2 Corn Husks
- 3 Slices Bacon, sliced
- 4 Can Cream of Potato Soup, Condensed
- 3 Cup whole milk
- 8 Ounce cream cheese
- 3 green onions, thinly sliced
- 2 Teaspoon hot sauce

Directions:

1. Supply your smoker with wood pellets and follow the start-up procedure. Preheat the grill, with the lid closed, to 180° F.

2. Sprinkle Traeger Fin & Feather rub as needed on salmon. Arrange the salmon skin-side down on the grill grate. Smoke for 30 minutes. Grill: 180 °F

3. Increase the grill temperature to 350°F. Grill: 350 °F

4. Cook the salmon for 30 minutes, or until the fish flakes easily with a fork. (The exact time will depend on the thickness of the fillet.) There is no need to turn the fish. Using a large thin spatula, transfer the salmon to a wire rack to cool. Remove the skin. (The salmon can be made a day ahead, wrapped in plastic wrap and refrigerated.) Break into flakes and set aside.

5. Arrange the corn and bacon strips on the grill grate. (The salmon will be roasting while you do this.) Roast the corn and the bacon until the corn is cooked through and browned in spots, turning as needed, and the bacon is crisp, about 15 minutes.

6. In the meantime, bring the cream of potato soup and the milk to a simmer over medium heat in a large saucepan or Dutch oven on the stovetop. Gradually stir in the cream cheese and whisk to blend. Chop the bacon into bits and slice the corn off the cobs using long strokes of a chef's knife.

7. Add to the soup along with the green onions. Stir in the salmon. Heat gently for 5 to 10 minutes. Add the hot sauce to taste. If the chowder is too thick, add more milk. Serve at once. Enjoy!

Hot-smoked Salmon

Servings: 4   Cooking Time: 180minutes

Ingredients:

- 1½lb (680g) skinless center-cut salmon fillet, preferably wild caught
- for the brine
- 1 quart (1 liter) distilled water

- ¼ cup coarse salt
- ¼ cup light brown sugar or low-carb equivalent
- ¼ cup gin (optional)

Directions:

1. In a saucepan on the stovetop over medium-high heat, make the brine by combining the water, salt, brown sugar, and gin (if using). Bring the mixture to a boil. Stir until the salt and sugar dissolve. Remove the pan from the stovetop and let the brine cool to room temperature. Refrigerate until cool.

2. Run your fingers over the salmon fillet, feeling for bones. Remove any with kitchen tweezers or needle-nosed pliers. Rinse the salmon under cold running water. Place the salmon in a resealable plastic bag and pour the brine over it. Refrigerate for 4 to 8 hours.

3. Place a wire rack on a rimmed sheet pan. Remove the salmon from the brine and rinse under cold running water. Pat dry with paper towels and then place the salmon on the wire rack. Place the pan in a cool area with good air circulation (such as near a fan). In 2 to 4 hours, you'll notice the salmon has developed a pellicle—a kind of sticky skin or coating that will help the smoke adhere to the fish. (Don't skip this step.)

4. Supply your smoker with wood pellets and follow the start-up procedure. Preheat the grill, with the lid closed, to 150° F.

5. Place the salmon on the grate and smoke until the fish flakes easily when pressed with a fork and the internal temperature reaches 140°F (60°C), about 3 hours. If albumin (a harmless white protein) appears on top of the fillet as it smokes, gently remove it with a paper towel.

6. Remove the salmon from the grill and let rest for 10 minutes. (You can also transfer the fish to a clean wire rack and let it cool to room temperature. Cover and refrigerate if not using immediately. The salmon will keep for up to 5 days.)

7. Serve the salmon with eggs, on salads, with Mustard Caviar, or with its traditional accompaniments: cream cheese, capers, chopped hard-boiled eggs, diced red onion, and dark bread.

Smoked Sugar Halibut

Servings: 8

Cooking Time: 120 Minutes

Ingredients:

- ➢ 1/4 cup granulated sugar
- ➢ 1/4 cup brown sugar
- ➢ 1/2 cup kosher salt
- ➢ 1 tsp ground coriander
- ➢ 2 lbs fresh halibut

Directions:

1. In a small bowl, mix the sugars, salt,and coriander together. Season the halibut on all sides.

2. Wrap the halibut in plastic wrap, place on a rimmed sheet pan,and brine in the fridge for 3 hours.

3. Remove the plastic wrap and rinse the fish. Pat it dry. Set it on a drying rack over a sheet pan for 1-2 hours in the fridge.

4. Supply your smoker with wood pellets and follow the start-up procedure. Preheat the grill, with the lid closed, to 200° F. Smoke the fish for 2 hours or until its internal temperature reaches 140 °F.

5. Serve your preferred sauce with the fish.

Grilled Salmon Steaks With Dill Sauce

Servings: 4

Cooking Time: 8 Minutes

Ingredients:

- 4 salmon steaks, each about 6 to 8oz (170 to 225g) and 1 inch (2.5cm) thick
- extra virgin olive oil
- coarse salt
- freshly ground rainbow peppercorns or freshly ground black pepper
- lemon wedges
- for the sauce
- 1 cup reduced-fat mayo
- ⅓ cup light sour cream
- ¼ cup chopped fresh dill
- 2 tbsp freshly squeezed lemon juice
- coarse salt
- freshly ground black pepper
- sprigs of fresh dill

Directions:

1. Supply your smoker with wood pellets and follow the start-up procedure. Preheat the grill, with the lid closed, to 450° F.

2. In a small bowl, make the dill sauce by combining the mayo, sour cream, dill, and lemon juice. Mix until smooth. Season with salt and pepper to taste. Transfer to a serving bowl. Scatter the dill sprigs over the top. Cover and refrigerate until ready to serve.

3. Brush the salmon with olive oil and season with salt and pepper. Place the salmon on the grate at an angle to the bars. Grill until grill marks begin to appear, about 4 minutes. Use a thin-bladed spatula to turn the salmon. Grill until the internal temperature reaches 140°F (60°C), about 4 minutes more.

4. Transfer the salmon to a platter. Serve immediately with the lemon wedges and dill sauce.

Delicious Smoked Trout

Servings: 8

Cooking Time: 120 Minutes

Ingredients:

- 6 rainbow trout fillets
- Brine:
- 2 Tablespoons kosher salt
- 2 Tablespoons brown sugar
- 4 cups cool water

Directions:

1. For the brine, dissolve the kosher salt and brown sugar in water.

2. Place the trout fillets in the brine, skin side up, and brine the fillets for 15 minutes.

3. Supply your smoker with wood pellets and follow the start-up procedure. Preheat the grill, with the lid closed, to 180° F.

4. Remove the trout from the brine and transfer it to the grill grates.

5. Smoke the trout for 1.5 to 2 hours with the lid closed, depending on the thickness of your fillets.

6. Smoke until the trout reaches an internal temperature of 145 °F, or until the trout flakes easily.

7. Remove the trout from the smoker and serve warm, or let it cool completely and serve chilled with your favorite accouterments.

Summer Paella

Servings: 6   Cooking Time: 45 Minutes

Ingredients:

- 6 tablespoons extra-virgin olive oil, divided, plus more for drizzling
- 2 green or red bell peppers, cored, seeded, and diced
- 2 medium onions, diced
- 2 garlic cloves, slivered
- 1 (29-ounce) can tomato purée
- 1½ pounds chicken thighs
- Kosher salt
- 1½ pounds tail-on shrimp, peeled and deveined
- 1 cup dried thinly sliced chorizo sausage
- 1 tablespoon smoked paprika
- 1½ teaspoons saffron threads
- 2 quarts chicken broth
- 3½ cups white rice
- 2 (7½-ounce) cans chipotle chiles in adobo sauce
- 1½ pounds fresh clams, soaked in cold water for 15 to 20 minutes2 tablespoons chopped fresh parsley
- 2 lemons, cut into wedges, for serving

Directions:

1. Make the sofrito: On the stove top, in a saucepan over medium-low heat, combine ¼ cup of olive oil, the bell peppers, onions, and garlic, and cook for 5 minutes, or until the onions are translucent.
2. Stir in the tomato purée, reduce the heat to low, and simmer, stirring frequently, until most of the liquid has evaporated, about 30 minutes. Set aside. (Note: The sofrito can be made in advance and refrigerated.)
3. Supply your smoker with wood pellets and follow the start-up procedure. Preheat, with the lid closed, to 450°F.
4. Heat a large paella pan on the smoker and add the remaining 2 tablespoons of olive oil.
5. Add the chicken thighs, season lightly with salt, and brown for 6 to 10 minutes, then push to the outer edge of the pan.
6. Add the shrimp, season with salt, close the lid, and smoke for 3 minutes.
7. Add the sofrito, chorizo, paprika, and saffron, and stir together.
8. In a separate bowl, combine the chicken broth, uncooked rice, and 1 tablespoon of salt, stirring until well combined.
9. Add the broth-rice mixture to the paella pan, spreading it evenly over the other ingredients.
10. Close the lid and smoke for 5 minutes, then add the chipotle chiles and clams on top of the rice.
11. Close the lid and continue to smoke the paella for about 30 minutes, or until all of the liquid is absorbed.

12. Remove the pan from the grill, cover tightly with aluminum foil, and let rest off the heat for 5 minutes.

13. Drizzle with olive oil, sprinkle with the fresh parsley, and serve with the lemon wedges.

Smoked Lobster Scampi

Servings: 2   Cooking Time: 30 Minutes

Ingredients:

- 1 Lobster Tail
- 1 Handful Pasta, Angel Hair
- 2 Tablespoon butter
- 1 Teaspoon garlic, minced
- 1/2 Teaspoon lemon juice
- 2 Teaspoon Parmesan cheese, grated
- 2 Tablespoon Sun Dried Tomato Pesto
- fresh parsley

Directions:

1. Supply your smoker with wood pellets and follow the start-up procedure. Preheat the grill, with the lid closed, to 180° F.

2. Use kitchen shears to cut along the top of the lobster on both sides to expose the meat. Place the lobster directly on the grill for 20-25 minutes, depending on the size of the lobster. Grill: 180 °F

3. While lobster smokes, cook pasta according to packaged directions.

4. After 20-25 minutes, take lobster off the grill and remove the meat from the tail. Cut meat into chunks.

5. While the pasta is boiling, melt butter over medium high heat. Once butter starts to brown, add the garlic and lobster chunks. Toss in pan a few times then add lemon and parmesan. Set aside.

6. When pasta has finished, place 1 tbsp of the sun dried tomato pesto on the bottom of a bowl or plate. Top with pasta, then finish with the lobster scampi. Garnish with parsley. Enjoy!

PORK RECIPES

Braised Pork Carnitas

Servings: 6

Cooking Time: 180 Minutes

Ingredients:

- 2 Tbsp Bacon Fat Or Olive Oil
- 1 Cup Chicken Stock
- Cilantro, Chopped
- Corn Tortillas
- 3 Jalapeno Pepper, Minced
- 1 Lime, Wedges
- 2 Tbsp Pulled Pork Rub
- 3 Lbs Pork Shoulder, Boneless, Cut Into 1 ½ To 2 Inch Cubes
- Queso Fresco, Crumbled
- Red Onion, Minced

Directions:

1. Supply your smoker with wood pellets and follow the start-up procedure. Preheat the grill, with the lid open, to 300° F. If using a gas or charcoal grill, set it up for medium-low heat.

2. Season cubed pork shoulder with Pulled Pork Rub, then transfer to a cast iron Dutch oven, and add chicken stock. Transfer to center of grill with sear slide open. Bring mixture to a boil, then cover and close the sear slide. Simmer pork for 2 ½ hours, until tender.

3. Remove the lid and open the sear slide. Bring to boil and reduce liquid by half, about 15 minutes. Remove from grill and set aside.

4. Heat 1 tablespoon of bacon fat in the skillet, then use a slotted spoon to transfer the pork to the skillet. Fry pork in fat, stirring occasionally, for 8 to 10 minutes, until pork crisps up. Remove from grill.

5. Serve pork carnitas warm in fresh corn tortillas, with cilantro, red onion, jalapeño, queso fresco, and fresh lime.

Jalapeño-bacon Pork Tenderloin

Servings: 4-6

Cooking Time: 150 Minutes

Ingredients:

- ¼ cup yellow mustard
- 2 (1-pound) pork tenderloins
- ¼ cup Pork Rub
- 8 ounces cream cheese, softened
- 1 cup grated Cheddar cheese
- 1 tablespoon unsalted butter, melted
- 1 tablespoon minced garlic
- 2 jalapeño peppers, seeded and diced
- 1½ pounds bacon

Directions:

1. Slather the mustard all over the pork tenderloins, then sprinkle generously with the dry rub to coat the meat.

2. Supply your smoker with wood pellets and follow the start-up procedure. Preheat, with the lid closed, to 225°F.

3. Place the tenderloins directly on the grill, close the lid, and smoke for 2 hours.

4. Remove the pork from the grill and increase the temperature to 375°F.

5. In a small bowl, combine the cream cheese, Cheddar cheese, melted butter, garlic, and jalapeños.

6. Starting from the top, slice deeply along the center of each tenderloin end to end, creating a cavity.

7. Spread half of the cream cheese mixture in the cavity of one tenderloin. Repeat with the remaining mixture and the other piece of meat.

8. Securely wrap one tenderloin with half of the bacon. Repeat with the remaining bacon and the other piece of meat.

9. Transfer the bacon-wrapped tenderloins to the grill, close the lid, and smoke for about 30 minutes, or until a meat thermometer inserted in the thickest part of the meat reads 160°F and the bacon is browned and cooked through.

10. Let the tenderloins rest for 5 to 10 minutes before slicing and serving.

Jalapeno Cheddar Smoked Sausages

Servings: 6

Cooking Time: 180 Minutes

Ingredients:

- hog casings
- 2 Pound ground pork
- 5 Medium jalapeños, seeded and diced small
- 1/2 Cup shredded sharp cheddar cheese
- 1/2 Tablespoon kosher salt
- 1 Teaspoon black pepper
- 1 Teaspoon granulated garlic
- 1 Teaspoon onion powder

Directions:

1. Soak your hog casings in water according to package directions. While casings are soaking, make your sausage.

2. Place all ingredients in the bowl of a food processor and pulse to combine. Be careful not to overwork, the meat should be a little tacky and all spices fully incorporated.

3. Place sausage mixture in your sausage stuffer and proceed to stuff the casing according to manufacturer's directions. Be sure to stuff the length of the casing, then create the links afterwards. Use caution not to overstuff or they will burst when you go to create the links.

4. Hang the sausages and allow to air dry at room temperature for an hour or so, then transfer to the refrigerator to dry overnight.

5. Supply your smoker with wood pellets and follow the start-up procedure. Preheat the grill, with the lid closed, to 180° F.

6. Place the sausages directly on the grill grate and smoke for 2 to 3 hours, or until they reach an internal temperature of 155°F. Enjoy! Grill: 180 °F Probe: 155 °F

Baked German Pork Schnitzel With Grilled Lemons

Servings: 2

Cooking Time: 20 Minutes

Ingredients:

- 16 Ounce pork chops
- salt
- black pepper
- 1 Teaspoon garlic powder
- 1 Teaspoon paprika
- 2 eggs
- 1 Cup panko breadcrumbs
- 1/2 Cup flour
- 2 Whole lemon, halved

Directions:

1. Supply your smoker with wood pellets and follow the start-up procedure. Preheat the grill, with the lid closed, to High heat.

2. Place pork chops individually between 2 pieces of plastic wrap. Pound with a meat mallet until they are around 1/4 to 1/8" thick. Season both sides generously with salt and black pepper.

3. Mix the garlic powder and paprika in a bowl. In another bowl whisk the eggs. In a third bowl add the breadcrumbs.

4. Dip pork cutlets one by one into flour shaking off any excess, then into eggs and then into the breadcrumbs. Place breaded pork cutlets onto a lightly oiled wire rack over a baking sheet.

5. Cook for 15 minutes then flip and bake for another 5 minutes. When you open the grill to flip pork place sliced lemons directly on grill grate flesh side down. Grill: 500 °F

6. Remove from grill and serve immediately with grilled lemons. Enjoy!

Bbq Sweet & Smoky Ribs

Servings: 6

Cooking Time: 300 Minutes

Ingredients:

➢ 2 Rack Pork, Spare Ribs Trimmed

➢ 6 Cup apple juice

➢ 2 Tablespoon Big Game Rub

➢ 2 Cup 'Que BBQ Sauce

➢ 1/4 Cup brown sugar

Directions:

1.   If your butcher has not already done so, remove the thin papery membrane from the bone-side of the ribs by working the tip of a butter knife underneath the membrane over a middle bone. Use paper towels to get a firm grip, then tear the membrane off.

2.   Lay the ribs in a baking dish. Pour the apple juice over ribs, using as much apple juice as needed to submerge the meaty side of the ribs. Turn to coat.

3.   Cover and refrigerate ribs for 4 to 6 hours or overnight. Remove the ribs from the apple juice; reserve juice.

4.   Sprinkle ribs on all sides with Traeger Big Game Rub.

5.   Supply your smoker with wood pellets and follow the start-up procedure. Preheat the grill, with the lid closed, to 225° F.

6.   Transfer the apple juice to a saucepan and place in a corner of the grill, the juice will keep the cooking environment moist.

7.   Arrange the ribs bone side down, directly on the grill grate. Cook for 4 to 5 hours, or until a skewer or paring knife inserted between the bones goes in easily.

8.   Check the internal temperature of the ribs, the desired temperature is 202℉. If not at temperature, cook for an additional 30 minutes or until temperature is reached.

9.   Meanwhile, combine the BBQ sauce and brown sugar in a small saucepan. Generously brush the ribs on all sides with the BBQ sauce the last hour of cooking

10. Using a sharp knife, cut the slabs into individual ribs. Serve. Enjoy!

Double-decker Pulled Pork Nachos With Smoked Cheese

Servings: 4

Cooking Time: 55 Minutes

Ingredients:

- 8 Ounce pepper jack cheese
- 8 Ounce Cheese, sharp cheddar
- tortilla chips
- 2 Cup leftover pulled pork
- black olives
- jalapeño, diced
- cilantro

Directions:

1. Supply your smoker with wood pellets and follow the start-up procedure. Preheat the grill, with the lid closed, to 165° F.

2. Place the cheese (frozen) on a rack on top of a tray filled with ice. You may want to cut the cheese into smaller portions, maybe 2 or 3 chunks per block, to help it smoke more quickly.

3. Smoke the cheeses for 45 to 60 minutes; allow to cool. Shred the cheeses (about 1 cup of each), and set aside. Grill: 165 °F

4. Turn the heat on the Traeger up to 350 degrees and preheat, lid closed, for 10 to 15 minutes. Grill: 350 °F

5. Lay out your tortilla chips on large baking sheet and top evenly with the shredded, smoked cheeses. Place the baking sheet on the Traeger grill grate and cook for about 10 minutes, or until the cheese is melted and bubbly. Grill: 350 °F

6. Remove the pan from the Traeger and start to assemble the double-decker nachos. Assemble the nachos with a layer of cheesy chips on the bottom, some pulled pork, and more cheesy chips on top. Finish it off with your favorite nacho toppings. Serve warm.

Pork Tenderloin With Bourbon Peaches

Servings: 6

Cooking Time: 27 Minutes

Ingredients:

- 2 pork tenderloins, about 2lb (1kg) total, trimmed of silver skin and excess fat
- extra virgin olive oil
- for the rub
- 3 tbsp coarse salt
- 3 tbsp freshly ground black pepper
- 3 tbsp smoked or regular paprika
- 3 tbsp granulated light brown sugar or low-carb substitute
- 2 tbsp instant coffee
- 1 tbsp granulated garlic
- 2 tsp ground cumin
- 1 tsp chili powder
- for the peaches
- 4 freestone peaches, about 1lb (450g) total, peeled, pitted, and sliced
- 1 tbsp freshly squeezed lemon juice
- ¼ cup unsalted butter
- 4 tbsp granulated light brown sugar or low-carb substitute
- 2 tbsp bourbon
- ½ tsp ground cinnamon
- ½ tsp pure vanilla extract
- pinch of coarse salt

Directions:

1. Supply your smoker with wood pellets and follow the start-up procedure. Preheat the grill, with the lid closed, to 400° F.

2. In a small bowl, make the rub by combining the ingredients. Coat the tenderloins in olive oil and season with the rub.

3. Place the peaches and lemon juice in a medium bowl, turning the peaches gently to coat. Measure the other ingredients and then take them and the peaches grill side.

4. Place 1 tablespoon of olive oil in the hot skillet and add the tenderloins. Quickly sear the pork, about 2 to 3 minute per side, turning as needed with tongs. When they're nicely browned, transfer the tenderloins to the grate. Cook until the internal temperature in the thickest part of the meat reaches 145°F (63°C), about 8 minutes. For moist meat, don't cook the tenderloins beyond 155°F (68°C).

5. Transfer the pork to a cutting board and tent with aluminum foil.

6. Replace the cast iron skillet with a clean one and close the grill lid to let it heat. Once hot, make the bourbon peaches by melting the butter. Add the brown sugar, bourbon, cinnamon, vanilla, and salt. Cook the mixture until it bubbles, about 5 to 8 minutes. Add the peaches and cook for 5 to 8 minutes more, turning the peaches carefully with a spoon to coat. Carefully transfer the skillet to a trivet or another heatproof surface.

7. Slice the pork on a diagonal into ½-inch (1.25cm) slices. Shingle the slices on a platter. Spoon the peaches around the pork or serve separately.

Bbq Bacon-wrapped Water Chestnuts

Servings: 6

Cooking Time: 35 Minutes

Ingredients:

- 1 Pound bacon
- 2 Can Water Chestnuts
- 1/3 Cup brown sugar
- 1/3 Cup mayonnaise
- 1/3 Cup Texas Spicy BBQ Sauce

Directions:

1. Supply your smoker with wood pellets and follow the start-up procedure. Preheat the grill, with the lid closed, to 350° F.

2. Line a rimmed baking sheet with aluminum foil. Cut each piece of bacon into thirds or halves. Wrap each water chestnut with a piece of bacon large enough to encircle it and secure the bacon with a toothpick.

3. Arrange the bacon-wrapped chestnuts in a single layer on the prepared baking sheet. Bake for 20 minutes. Leave the grill on. Grill: 350 °F

4. Meanwhile, whisk the mayonnaise, brown sugar, and Traeger Spicy Barbecue Sauce in a mixing bowl. Pour the sauce over the chestnuts and return to the grill to bake for 10 to 15 minutes more. Transfer to a platter for serving. Enjoy!

Maple Syrup Bacon Wrapped Tenderloin

Servings: 5

Cooking Time: 30 Minutes

Ingredients:

➢ 1 Package Bacon, Thick Cut

➢ 1/4 Cup Maple Syrup

➢ 2 Tbsp Olive Oil

➢ 3 Tbsp Competition Smoked Rub

➢ 1 Trimmed With Silver Skin Removed Pork, Tenderloin

Directions:

1. Lay the strips of bacon out flat, with each strip slightly overlapping the other.

2. Sprinkle the pork tenderloin with 1 tablespoon of the Competition Smoked Rub and lay in the center.

3. Wrap with bacon over the tenderloin and tuck in the ends.

4. In a small bowl, mix the olive oil, maple syrup and remaining seasoning together and brush onto the wrapped tenderloin.

5. Supply your smoker with wood pellets and follow the start-up procedure. Preheat the grill, with the lid open, to 350° F.

6. When the grill is ready, place your tenderloin on the grill and cook, turning, for 15 minutes.

7. Increase the grill temperature to 400°F and grill for another 15 minutes or until the internal temperature is 145°F. Serve and enjoy!

Baked Sage & Sausage Stuffing

Servings: 4

Cooking Time: 45 Minutes

Ingredients:

- 1 Pound Sage-Flavored Sausage, Such as Bob Evans Or Jimmy Dean
- 1/2 Cup onion, diced
- 1/2 Cup celery, diced
- 14 Ounce (14 oz) package herb seasoned stuffing
- 1/2 Cup dried sweetened cranberries
- 2 Cup low sodium chicken broth
- 6 Tablespoon butter
- butter

Directions:

1. Brown the sausage in a large frying pan, breaking up the sausage with a wooden spoon.

2. Add the onion and celery and cook until softened. Drain any excess fat. Transfer to a large mixing bowl. Add the stuffing mix and cranberries, if using.

3. Warm the chicken broth over medium-low heat; add butter and cook until melted. Toss with the bread/sausage mixture and mix lightly.

4. Butter a 3-qt casserole or baking dish. Do not compress the mixture or it will be dense.

5. Supply your smoker with wood pellets and follow the start-up procedure. Preheat the grill, with the lid closed, to 350° F.

6. Bake the stuffing, covered, for 35 to 45 minutes; uncover during the last 20 minutes of cooking if you prefer a crunchier texture. Grill: 350 ˚F

7. Remove from grill and serve. Enjoy!

Pulled Pork Sliders Hawaiian Rolls

Servings: 6 - 8

Cooking Time: 5 Minutes

Ingredients:

- ½ Cup Apple Cider Vinegar
- 1 Package Of Cabbage
- 2 Tbsp Minced Cilantro
- 1/3 Cup Green Onions, Diced
- 1 Tbsp Mango Magic
- 1 ½ Cup Mayonnaise
- 1 Cup Pineapple, Diced
- 1 Lbs Pulled Pork
- 8 Hawaiian Rolls

Directions:

1. In a large bowl mix together all of the coleslaw ingredients and let set in refrigerator for at least 2 hours.

2. Reheat the pulled pork in a microwave or grill.

3. Serve over the pulled pork on the Hawaiian rolls.

Pork & Pepperoni Burgers

Servings: 4

Cooking Time: 60 Minutes

Ingredients:

- 1lb (450g) bulk pork sausage, preferably Italian
- 1lb (450g) ground pork, well chilled
- 8 slices of bacon, preferably thick-cut
- 8oz (225g) grated mozzarella cheese, plus more
- 1 tsp Italian seasoning
- ½ cup pizza sauce
- 1½oz (40g) pepperoni, roughly chopped

Directions:

1. Wet your hands with cold water. In a large bowl, combine the sausage and ground pork until well mixed. Line a rimmed sheet pan with aluminum foil. Divide the meat into 4 equal-sized balls and place on the sheet pan. Spray the lower third of a soda can (including the bottom) with cooking spray. Firmly press the can into one of the meatballs to create a meat bowl with uniform sides. Gently twist or rock the can to remove. Use your hands to repair any cracks in the bowl.

2. Wrap 2 slices of bacon around the circumference of the bowl and secure with toothpicks. Repeat with the remaining meatballs, respraying the can with cooking spray as necessary. Chill for 1 hour.

3. Supply your smoker with wood pellets and follow the start-up procedure. Preheat the grill, with the lid closed, to 300° F.

4. Place the patties cup side up on the grate and grill for 30 minutes. Use paper towels to blot any grease that pools at the bottom of the cups.

5. Sprinkle 2 tablespoons of cheese into each cup. Top each patty with equal amounts of Italian seasoning, pizza sauce, and pepperoni. Generously sprinkle more cheese over the top. Continue to grill until the bacon crisps, the cheese melts, and the internal temperature reaches 160°F (71°C), about 20 to 30 minutes more.

6. Remove the burgers from the grill and rest for 3 minutes. Remove the toothpicks and serve immediately.

VEGETABLES RECIPES

Traeger Grilled Whole Corn

Servings: 4

Cooking Time: 25 Minutes

Ingredients:

- 3 green onions
- 6 Tablespoon butter, softened
- 1 Teaspoon chile powder
- 1 Teaspoon toasted sesame seeds
- 4 ears corn, in husk

Directions:

1. Supply your smoker with wood pellets and follow the start-up procedure. Preheat the grill, with the lid closed, to 325° F.

2. Place green onions directly on the grill grate and cook 15 minutes until lightly charred. Remove from grill and set aside.

3. Sesame-Chile Butter: Take butter out of fridge and let soften. Chop up charred green onions and add to butter along with chile powder and sesame seeds. Mash all ingredients together.

4. Grill corn, rotating occasionally, until husks are blackened (some will flake and fall off) and kernels are tender with some browned and charred spots, about 25 to 35 minutes. Grill: 325 ˚F

5. Let corn cool slightly, then shuck. Serve with the Sesame-Chile Butter. Enjoy

Grilled Zucchini Squash Spears

Servings: 4

Cooking Time: 10 Minutes

Ingredients:

- 4 Medium zucchini
- 2 Tablespoon olive oil
- 1 Tablespoon sherry vinegar
- 2 thyme, leaves pulled
- salt and pepper

Directions:

1. Clean the zucchini and cut the ends off. Cut each in half lengthwise, then each half into thirds.

2. Combine remaining ingredients in a medium Ziplock bag and add the spears. Toss and mix well to coat the zucchini.

3. Supply your smoker with wood pellets and follow the start-up procedure. Preheat the grill, with the lid closed, to 350° F.

4. Remove the spears from the bag and place directly on the grill grate cut side down.

5. Cook for 3-4 minutes per side, until grill marks appear and zucchini is tender. Grill: 350 °F

6. Remove from grill and finish with more thyme leaves if desired. Enjoy!

Baked Winter Squash Au Gratin

Servings: 8

Cooking Time: 45 Minutes

Ingredients:

- 2 Cup heavy cream
- salt and pepper
- 3 Cup shredded Gruyere cheese
- 4 Clove garlic, diced
- 2 Tablespoon butter
- 3 yellow potatoes, peeled and cubed
- 1 butternut squash seeded, peeled and cubed
- 1 acorn squash seeded, peeled and cubed

Directions:

1. Supply your smoker with wood pellets and follow the start-up procedure. Preheat the grill, with the lid closed, to 375° F.

2. In a medium saucepan, cook the cream, stirring constantly, until it comes to a low boil. Add salt, pepper, garlic and shredded Gruyere cheese. Stir until cheese is melted.

3. Grease a 9x13 inch baking dish with 2 tablespoons of butter. In a large mixing bowl, combine potatoes, butternut and acorn squash. Stir in the cheese sauce. Place mixture in the prepared baking dish and place in grill.

4. Cook for 45 minutes or until potatoes and squash are fork tender. Remove from grill and let cool for 10 minutes before serving. Enjoy! Grill: 375 °F

Blt Pasta Salad

Servings: 6

Cooking Time: 45 Minutes

Ingredients:

- 1 pound thick-cut bacon
- 16 ounces bowtie pasta, cooked according to package directions and drained
- 2 tomatoes, chopped
- ½ cup chopped scallions
- ½ cup Italian dressing
- ½ cup ranch dressing
- 1 tablespoon chopped fresh basil
- 1 teaspoon salt
- 1 teaspoon freshly ground black pepper
- 1 teaspoon garlic powder
- 1 head lettuce, cored and torn

Directions:

1. Supply your smoker with wood pellets and follow the start-up procedure. Preheat, with the lid closed, to 225°F.

2. Arrange the bacon slices on the grill grate, close the lid, and cook for 30 to 45 minutes, flipping after 20 minutes, until crisp.

3. Remove the bacon from the grill and chop.

4. In a large bowl, combine the chopped bacon with the cooked pasta, tomatoes, scallions, Italian dressing, ranch dressing, basil, salt, pepper, and garlic powder. Refrigerate until ready to serve.

5. Toss in the lettuce just before serving to keep it from wilting.

Tater Tot Bake

Servings: 4

Cooking Time: 15 Minutes

Ingredients:

- 1 Whole frozen tater tots
- salt and pepper
- 1 Cup sour cream
- 1 Cup shredded cheddar cheese, divided
- 1/2 Cup bacon, chopped
- 1/4 Cup green onion, diced

Directions:

1. Supply your smoker with wood pellets and follow the start-up procedure. Preheat the grill, with the lid closed, to 375° F.

2. Line a baking sheet with aluminum foil for easy clean up and spread frozen tater tots onto sheet.

3. Sprinkle with Veggie Shake or salt and pepper to taste.

4. Place the baking sheet on the preheated grill grate and cook the tater tots for 10 minutes.

5. Drizzle sour cream over cooked tater tots.

6. Sprinkle the cheese, bacon bits and green onions on top of the tater tots.

7. Turn heat up to High heat and cook for 5 more minutes until the cheese melts and serve immediately. Enjoy!

Roasted Jalapeño Poppers

Servings: 2

Cooking Time: 30 Minutes

Ingredients:

- 8 Slices Bacon, Center Cut
- 2 Cup cream cheese
- 2 Ounce Cheese, sharp cheddar
- 1/2 Cup green onions, minced
- 2 Teaspoon fresh squeezed lime juice
- 4 Tablespoon Seeded Tomato, Chopped
- 4 Tablespoon cilantro, chopped
- 1/2 Teaspoon kosher salt
- 2 Small garlic clove, minced
- 12 Whole Jalapeños

Directions:

1. Supply your smoker with wood pellets and follow the start-up procedure. Preheat the grill, with the lid closed, to 350° F.

2. Place 2 bacon slices directly on the grill grate and cook 10-15 minutes until cooked through and crispy flipping halfway through. Remove from grill, but leave the grill on. When cool enough to handle, coarsely chop the bacon and reserve. Grill: 350 ˚F

3. In the bowl of a stand mixer, combine cream cheese, cheddar cheese, green onions, chopped bacon, lime juice, tomatoes, cilantro, salt and garlic. Mix on medium speed with a paddle until combined. Transfer mixture to a piping bag.

4. Cut the tops off the jalapeños and remove the seeds and ribs with a small paring knife.

5. Pipe the filling into each pepper so that the filling comes up a 1/4" over the top of the pepper. Place the tops back on each pepper.

6. With a rolling pin, flatten out the remaining six slices of bacon until they are 1/8" thick. Cut each slice in half. Wrap 1/2 a bacon slice around each pepper and secure with a toothpick.

7. Place the peppers in the Traeger Jalapeno Popper Tray. Place the tray directly on the grill grate and cook for 30-40 minutes until the peppers are tender, bacon is crispy, and cheese is melted. Enjoy! Grill: 350 ˚F

Potluck Salad With Smoked Cornbread

Servings: 6

Cooking Time: 45 Minutes

Ingredients:

- 1 cup all-purpose flour
- 1 cup yellow cornmeal
- 1 tablespoon sugar
- 2 teaspoons baking powder
- 1 teaspoon salt
- 1 cup milk
- 1 egg, beaten, at room temperature
- 4 tablespoons (½ stick) unsalted butter, melted and cooled
- Nonstick cooking spray or butter, for greasing
- ½ cup milk
- ½ cup sour cream
- 2 tablespoons dry ranch dressing mix
- 1 pound bacon, cooked and crumbled
- 3 tomatoes, chopped
- 1 bell pepper, chopped
- 1 cucumber, seeded and chopped
- 2 stalks celery, chopped (about 1 cup)
- ½ cup chopped scallions

Directions:

1. For the cornbread:
2. In a medium bowl, combine the flour, cornmeal, sugar, baking powder, and salt.
3. In a small bowl, whisk together the milk and egg. Pour in the butter, then slowly fold this mixture into the dry ingredients.
4. Supply your smoker with wood pellets and follow the start-up procedure. Preheat, with the lid closed, to 375°F.
5. Coat a cast iron skillet with cooking spray or butter.
6. Pour the batter into the skillet, place on the grill grate, close the lid, and smoke for 35 to 45 minutes, or until the cornbread is browned and pulls away from the side of the skillet.
7. Remove the cornbread from the grill and let cool, then coarsely crumble.
8. For the salad:
9. In a small bowl, whisk together the milk, sour cream, and ranch dressing mix.
10. In a medium bowl, combine the crumbled bacon, tomatoes, bell pepper, cucumber, celery, and scallions.
11. In a large serving bowl, layer half of the crumbled cornbread, half of the bacon-veggie mixture, and half of the dressing. Toss lightly.
12. Repeat the layering with the remaining cornbread, bacon-veggie mixture, and dressing. Toss again.
13. Refrigerate the salad for at least 1 hour. Serve cold.

Roasted Mashed Potatoes

Servings: 8

Cooking Time: 40 Minutes

Ingredients:

- 5 Pound Yukon Gold potatoes
- 1 1/2 Stick butter, softened
- 1 1/2 Cup heavy whipping cream, room temperature
- kosher salt
- white pepper

Directions:

1. Supply your smoker with wood pellets and follow the start-up procedure. Preheat the grill, with the lid closed, to 300° F.

2. Peel and cut potatoes into 1/2 inch cubes. Place the potatoes in a shallow baking dish with 1/2 cup water and cover. Bake until tender, about 40 minutes. Grill: 300 ℉

3. In a medium saucepan, combine cream and butter. Cook over medium heat until butter is melted.

4. Remove potatoes from the grill and drain water.

5. Transfer potatoes to a bowl and mash using a potato masher. Gradually add in cream and butter mixture and mix using the masher. Be careful not to overwork or the potatoes will becomes gluey. Season with salt and pepper to taste. Enjoy!

Smoked Parmesan Herb Popcorn

Servings: 2

Cooking Time: 15 Minutes

Ingredients:

➢ 4 Tablespoon butter

➢ 2 Teaspoon Italian Seasoning

➢ 1 Teaspoon garlic powder

➢ 1 Teaspoon salt

➢ 1/4 Cup popcorn kernels

➢ 1/2 Cup Parmesan cheese, grated

Directions:

1. Supply your smoker with wood pellets and follow the start-up procedure. Preheat the grill, with the lid closed, to 250° F.

2. In a small saucepan, melt the butter over medium heat. Add Italian seasoning, garlic powder, and salt and stir to combine. Remove from heat and set aside.

3. Add 1/4 cup of popcorn to a brown paper lunch bag. Fold the top of the bag over twice to close. Place the bag in the microwave and microwave on high for 1 to 2 minutes, or until there are about 5 seconds between pops. Open the bag with care and dump into a large mixing bowl.

4. Pour butter mixture of popcorn in a bowl and toss to combine. Dump popcorn onto a baking sheet and place in grill.

5. Smoke for 10 minutes; remove from grill. Toss with parmesan cheese to serve. Enjoy! Grill: 250 °F

Grilled Broccoli Rabe

Servings: 4

Cooking Time: 10 Minutes

Ingredients:

- 4 Tablespoon extra-virgin olive oil
- 4 Bunch broccoli rabe or broccolini
- kosher salt
- 1 lemon, halved

Directions:

1. Supply your smoker with wood pellets and follow the start-up procedure. Preheat the grill, with the lid closed, to 450° F.

2. On a platter or in a mixing bowl, drizzle the olive oil over the broccoli rabe. Use your hands to mix thoroughly, coating the vegetables evenly with the oil. Season with sea salt.

3. Place the broccoli rabe in one layer directly on the lowest grill grate. Close the lid and cook for 5 to 10 minutes. You want there to be some color and slight char on the first side. Flip and cook for a few more minutes. Grill: 450 ˚F

4. Transfer the broccoli rabe to a serving platter and squeeze the juice of half a lemon evenly over the top.

5. Serve with more lemon wedges on the side. Enjoy!

Traeger Smoked Coleslaw

Servings: 8

Cooking Time: 20 Minutes

Ingredients:

- 1 Head purple cabbage, shredded
- 1 Head green cabbage, shredded
- 1 Cup shredded carrots
- 2 scallions, thinly sliced
- 1 1/2 Cup mayonnaise
- 1/8 Cup white wine vinegar
- 1 Teaspoon celery seed
- 1 Teaspoon sugar
- salt and pepper

Directions:

1. Supply your smoker with wood pellets and follow the start-up procedure. Preheat the grill, with the lid closed, to 180° F.

2. Spread cabbage and carrots out on a sheet tray and place directly on the grill grates. Smoke for 20 to 25 minutes or until cabbage picks up desired amount of smoke. Grill: 180 °F

3. Remove from grill and transfer to the refrigerator immediately to cool. While cabbage is cooling, make the dressing.

4. For the dressing, combine all ingredients in a small bowl and mix well.

5. Place smoked cabbage and carrots in a large bowl and pour dressing over them. Stir to coat well.

6. Transfer to a serving dish and sprinkle with scallions. Enjoy!

Roasted Sheet Pan Vegetables

Servings: 4

Cooking Time: 25 Minutes

Ingredients:

- 1 Small head purple cauliflower, stemmed and cut into 2 inch florets
- 1 Small head yellow cauliflower, stemmed and cut into 2 inch florets
- 4 Cup butternut squash
- 2 Cup oyster or shiitake mushrooms, rinsed and sliced
- 3 Tablespoon olive oil
- 2 Teaspoon kosher salt
- freshly ground black pepper
- 1/4 Cup chopped flat-leaf parsley

Directions:

1. Supply your smoker with wood pellets and follow the start-up procedure. Preheat the grill, with the lid closed, to 450° F.

2. In a large mixing bowl, combine all of the vegetables. Drizzle olive oil over the top, along with kosher salt and a generous grinding of black pepper.

3. Using your hands, toss the vegetables until they are evenly coated.

4. Spread out onto 1 or 2 half sheet pans or baking sheets, ensuring there is a little space between the veggies. (If they are too crowded, the vegetables will steam instead of roast and you won't get that crispy texture.)

5. Place the sheet pans on the grill and cook for 15 minutes. Open and stir, then close the lid and continue to cook until the vegetables are brown around the edges, about 5 to 15 minutes longer. Grill: 450 °F

6. Toss with parsley and serve immediately. The vegetables are also delicious at room temperature. Enjoy!

POULTRY RECIPES

Smoking Duck With Mandarin Glaze

Servings: 4   Cooking Time: 240 Minutes

Ingredients:

- 1 quart buttermilk
- 1 (5-pound) whole duck
- ¾ cup soy sauce
- ½ cup hoisin sauce
- ½ cup rice wine vinegar

- 2 tablespoons sesame oil
- 1 tablespoon freshly ground black pepper
- 1 tablespoon minced garlic
- Mandarin Glaze, for drizzling

Directions:

1. With a very sharp knife, remove as much fat from the duck as you can. Refrigerate or freeze the fat for later use.

2. Pour the buttermilk into a large container with a lid and submerge the whole duck in it. Cover and let brine in the refrigerator for 4 to 6 hours.

3. Supply your smoker with wood pellets and follow the start-up procedure. Preheat, with the lid closed, to 250°F.

4. Remove the duck from the buttermilk brine, then rinse it and pat dry with paper towels.

5. In a bowl, combine the soy sauce, hoisin sauce, vinegar, sesame oil, pepper, and garlic to form a paste. Reserve ¼ cup for basting.

6. Poke holes in the skin of the duck and rub the remaining paste all over and inside the cavity.

7. Place the duck on the grill breast-side down, close the lid, and smoke for about 4 hours, basting every hour with the reserved paste, until a meat thermometer inserted in the thickest part of the meat reads 165°F. Use aluminum foil to tent the duck in the last 30 minutes or so if it starts to brown too quickly.

8. To finish, drizzle with glaze.

Marinated Grilled Honey Chicken Wings

Servings: 4-6

Cooking Time: 30 Minutes

Ingredients:

- 1/2 Bottle Beer, Any Brand
- 2 Lbs Chicken Wings, Whole
- 2 Tablespoon Honey
- 1 Tablespoon Sweet Heat Rub
- 2 Tablespoon Rice Wine Vinegar
- 1/2 Tablesoon Sesame Oil
- 1/4 Cup Soy Sauce
- 1 Tablespoon Sriracha Hot Sauce

Directions:

1. In a large glass or plastic bowl, combine the beer, soy sauce, honey, rice wine vinegar, sriracha, sesame oil and   Sweet Heat Seasoning. Whisk well to combine.

2. Add the chicken wings to the marinade and toss well to combine. Cover with plastic wrap and refrigerate for 2 hours and up to 24 hours.

3. Remove chicken wings from refrigerator, drain marinade and pat dry. Supply your smoker with wood pellets and follow the start-up procedure. Supply your smoker with wood pellets and follow the start-up procedure. Preheat the grill, with the lid open, to 350° F. Place the wings on a grill pan and grill for 20-25 minutes, or until the wings' internal temperature is 165F. Remove from the grill, serve and enjoy!

Whole Smoked Honey Chicken

Servings: 4

Cooking Time: 40 Minutes

Ingredients:

- 1 Tablespoon Honey
- 1 ½ Lemon
- 4 Tablespoons   Champion Chicken Seasoning
- 4 Tablespoons Unsalted Butter
- 1, 4 Pound Chicken, Giblets Removed And Patted Dry

Directions:

1. Supply your smoker with wood pellets and follow the start-up procedure. Preheat the grill, with the lid open, to 225° F.

2. In a small saucepan, melt together the butter and honey over low heat. Squeeze ½ lemon into the honey mixture and remove from the heat.

3. Smoke the chicken, skin side down until the chicken is lightly browned and the skin releases from the grate without ripping, about 6-8 minutes.

4. Turn the chicken over and baste with the honey butter mixture.

5. Continue to smoke the chicken, basting every 45 minutes, until the thickest part of the chicken reaches 160°F.

Herb Roasted Turkey

                                    Cooking Time: 180 Minutes

Ingredients:

- 8 Tablespoon butter, room temperature
- 2 Tablespoon chopped mixed herbs, such as parsley, sage, rosemary and/or marjoram
- 1/4 Teaspoon black pepper
- 1 Teaspoon kosher salt
- 1 (12-14 lb) turkey, fresh or thawed
- 3 Tablespoon butter, melted
- Pork & Poultry Rub
- 2 Cup chicken or turkey broth

Directions:

1. In a small mixing bowl, combine the 8 tablespoons of softened butter, mixed herbs, salt and black pepper and beat until fluffy with a wooden spoon. (You can make the herbed butter several days ahead: Cover and refrigerate, but bring to room temperature before using).

2. Remove any giblets from the turkey cavity and save them for gravy making, if desired. Wash the turkey, inside and out, under cold running water. Dry with paper towels.

3. Place the turkey on a roasting rack in a roasting pan. Tuck the wings behind the back, and tie the legs together with butcher's string.

4. Using your fingers or the handle of a wooden spoon, gently push some of the herbed butter underneath the turkey skin onto the breast halves, being careful not to tear the skin. Massage the skin to evenly distribute the herbed butter. Rub the outside of the turkey with the melted butter and sprinkle with the Traeger Pork and Poultry Rub.

5. Pour the chicken broth in the bottom of the roasting pan.

6. Supply your smoker with wood pellets and follow the start-up procedure. Preheat the grill, with the lid closed, to 325° F.

7. Put the roasting pan with the turkey directly on the grill grate. Roast the turkey for 3 hours. Insert the probe from the meat thermometer in the thickest part of the thigh, but not touching bone. Cook until internal temperature reaches 165°F. The turkey should also be beautifully browned with crisp skin. If the temperature is less than that, or if your turkey is not browned to your liking, let it roast for another 30 minutes, then check the temperature again. Repeat until the turkey is fully cooked. Grill: 325 °F Probe: 165 °F

8. When the turkey is done, carefully transfer it to a cutting board and let it rest for 20 to 30 minutes. Do not tent it with aluminum foil or the skin will lose its crispness. Use the drippings that have accumulated in the bottom of the roasting pan to make gravy, if desired. Carve the turkey and serve.

Smoked Chicken Fajita Quesadillas

Servings: 4

Cooking Time: 45 Minutes

Ingredients:

- 2 Chicken, Boneless/Skinless
- 1 Tsp Chilli, Powder
- 1 Tsp Garlic Powder
- 1/2 Green Bell Pepper, Sliced
- 1 Cup Mexican Cheese, Shredded
- 1/2 Onion, Sliced
- 1/2 Tsp Oregano
- 1 Tsp Paprika, Powder
- 1/4 Tsp Pepper
- 1/2 Red Bell Peppers
- Salsa
- Sour Cream
- 4 Tortilla
- 1/2 Yellow Bell Pepper, Sliced

Directions:

1. Supply your smoker with wood pellets and follow the start-up procedure. Preheat the grill, with the lid open, to 350° F.

2. Combine spices in a bowl and season chicken breasts. Leave a little bit of seasoning for the vegetables.

3. Place chicken on the grates and cook for 30 minutes, flipped halfway through.

4. In a Vegetable Basket, combine all vegetables and season with the remaining spice mixture.

5. Open up the flame broiler and saute over the open flame for about 15 minutes, or until the vegetables are cooked to your liking.

6. On a tortilla, layer cheese, vegetables, sliced chicken and more cheese. Fold the tortilla and place over the open flame on your Grill. Sear until the tortilla is nicely toasted and the cheese is melted. Cut and serve with salsa and sour cream.

Savory Jerk Chicken Wings

Servings: 4

Cooking Time: 20 Minutes

Ingredients:

- 1 Tsp Allspice, Ground
- 3 Lbs Chicken Wings, Split
- 1/2 Tsp Cinnamon, Ground
- 4 Garlic Cloves, Smashed
- 2 Tsp Ginger, Grated
- 1 Habanero Pepper, Chopped
- 2 Tbsp Honey
- 2 Tbsp Lemon Juice
- 1/3 Cup Lime Juice
- 1/2 Tsp Nutmeg, Ground
- 1/2 Cup Olive Oil
- 1/4 Cup Poblano Pepper, Chopped
- 1 Tbsp Tamari
- 2 Tsp Thyme, Dried
- 1/2 Cup Yellow Onion, Chopped

Directions:

1. Add chicken to a large resealable plastic bag.

2. In the bowl of a food processor, add the garlic, onion, ginger, peppers, tamari, honey, lime juice, lemon juice, thyme, allspice, cinnamon, nutmeg, and oil. Process on low for 1 minute, then transfer marinade to the bag. Seal the bag and place in the refrigerator for at least 2 hours, up to overnight.

3. Supply your smoker with wood pellets and follow the start-up procedure. Preheat the grill, with the lid open, to 425° F. If using a gas or charcoal grill, set it up for medium-high heat.

4. Remove wings from the marinade, and discard remaining marinade. Place wings on the grill and cook for 15 to 20 minutes, flipping every 5 minutes, until an internal temperature of 165 F is reached.

5. Remove wings from the grill and serve warm.

Smoked Thanksgiving Turkey

Servings: 6 - 8

Cooking Time: 300 Minutes

Ingredients:

➢ 1 Turkey Brining Kits

➢ 12 – 14 Lbs Turkey

➢ 1 Gallon Water, Cold

➢ 4 Cups + 1 Gallon Water, Warm

Directions:

1. Start by defrosting the turkey overnight in the refrigerator.

2. Once turkey has been defrosted begin to make the brine by adding 4 cups of water and the brine mixture to a large stockpot.

3. Bring the mixture to a boil and add 1 gallon of cold water.

4. Place the turkey in the brine bag and pour the brine mixture over the turkey and refrigerate 1 hour per pound.

5. Once turkey has been brined rinse the turkey with cold water and set on a pan.

6. Using the seasoning in the brine box, season the turkey. Once turkey has been seasoned, supply your smoker with wood pellets and follow the start-up procedure. Preheat the grill, with the lid closed, to 275° F.

7. Place your turkey in the smoker and place the temperature probe in the deepest part of the breast. Cook at 275 until the breast and thigh meat internal temperature has reached 165°F to 170°F.

8. Remove the turkey from the smoker, let cool, and cut the turkey into your desired pieces. Enjoy!

Apricot Glazed Ham

Servings: 8

Cooking Time: 60 Minutes

Ingredients:

- 1 Cup Apricot Preserves
- 1/2 Cup apricot brandy
- 1/4 Cup honey
- 1/4 Cup brown sugar, firmly packed
- 1/4 Teaspoon ground cloves
- 6 Ounce Apricot Nectar, bottled or ginger ale
- 1 Large ham
- fresh parsley
- apricot, halved

Directions:

1. Supply your smoker with wood pellets and follow the start-up procedure. Preheat the grill, with the lid closed, to 325° F.

2. In a saucepan, stir together the apricot preserves, apricot brandy, honey, brown sugar, cloves, and apricot nectar and simmer over medium heat until the preserves, honey, and brown sugar have melted. Set aside and keep warm.

3. Place ham in large roasting pan lined with aluminum foil. Place pan on grill and cook for 1.5 hours.

4. Open Grill and glaze ham with reserved mixture. Continue cooking for another 30 minutes or until a thermometer is inserted into the thickest part of the meat and reaches an internal temperatures of 135 degrees F. Probe: 135 °F

5. Garnish the platter with the parsley and apricots, if desired. Enjoy!

Smoked Drumsticks

Servings: 2-4

Cooking Time: 25 Minutes

Ingredients:

- 1 pound chicken drumsticks
- 2 tablespoons olive oil
- 1 batch Sweet and Spicy Cinnamon Rub

Directions:

1. Supply your smoker with wood pellets and follow the start-up procedure. Preheat the grill, with the lid closed, to 350°F.

2. Coat the drumsticks all over with olive oil and season with the rub. Using your hands, work the rub into the meat.

3. Place the drumsticks directly on the grill grate and smoke until their internal temperature reaches 170°F. Remove the drumsticks from the grill and serve immediately.

Spicy Bbq Whole Chicken

Servings: 4

Cooking Time: 180 Minutes

Ingredients:

- 6 Thai chiles
- 2 Tablespoon sweet paprika
- 1 Scotch bonnet pepper
- 2 Tablespoon sugar
- 3 Tablespoon salt
- 1 white onion
- 5 Clove garlic
- 4 Cup grapeseed oil
- 1 whole chicken

Directions:

1. In a food processor or blender, puree the Thai chiles, paprika, Scotch bonnet pepper, sugar, salt, onion, garlic and grapeseed oil together until smooth.

2. Smother the chicken with mixture and let rest in fridge overnight.

3. Supply your smoker with wood pellets and follow the start-up procedure. Preheat the grill, with the lid closed, to 300° F.

4. Place chicken on grill, breast side up and smoke for 3 hours, or until it reaches an internal temperature of 165°F in the breast. Grill: 300 °F Probe: 165 °F

5. Remove from grill and allow to rest for 10 to 15 minutes before slicing. Serve with sides of choice. Enjoy!

Teriyaki Apple Cider Turkey

Servings: 8-10

Cooking Time: 180 Minutes

Ingredients:

- 1/2 Cup Apple Cider
- 1/4 Cup Melted Butter, Unsalted
- 1 Teaspoon Cornstarch
- 2 Finely Chopped Garlic, Cloves
- 1/2 Teaspoon Ginger, Ground
- 2 Tablespoon Honey
- 2 Tablespoon   Champion Chicken Seasoning
- 1 Shady Brook Farms® Whole Turkey, Thawed
- 2 Tablespoon Soy Sauce
- 1 Tablespoon Water, Cold

Directions:

1. Supply your smoker with wood pellets and follow the start-up procedure. Preheat the grill, with the lid closed, to 300° F.

2. In a saucepan, whisk together melted butter, garlic, soy sauce, apple cider, ground ginger, and honey. Bring to a boil then reduce to a simmer.

3. Place the turkey in an aluminum roasting pan.

4. With a marinade injector, fill with the mixture and pierce the meat with the needle while pushing on the plunger, injecting the flavor. You want to inject into the thickest part of the breast, thigh, and wings.

5. Next, rub entire turkey with your favorite poultry seasoning or the   Champion Chicken seasoning. For added flavor, throw some extra garlic gloves into the cavity and apple cider in the aluminum pan.

6. Place the turkey in the grill and cook until the internal temperature reaches 165-170°F.

7. In a separate bowl, mix cornstarch and cold water together and add to the leftover original mixture to create a glaze. Glaze the turkey with the remaining mixture with approximately 15-20 minutes left. Skin will darken because of the sugar in the glaze.

8. Let the turkey rest 20-25 minutes before carving and enjoy!

Onion Turkey Burger Sliders

Servings: 5

Cooking Time: 30 Minutes

Ingredients:

- 1 Sweet Onion, Chopped
- 1 Pepper, Anaheim
- Bacon Cheddar Burger Seasoning
- Spinach
- 16 Oz Turkey, Ground

Directions:

1. Supply your smoker with wood pellets and follow the start-up procedure. Preheat the grill, with the lid closed, to 400° F.

2. Put the ground turkey into a bowl and generously add the Bacon Cheddar Burger seasoning to the mixture.

3. Dice the Anaheim pepper and add it to the bowl as well.

4. Dice about 1/3 of the sweet onion and add it to the bowl.

5. Mix with your hands until the meat looks evenly coated in seasoning and the veggies are evenly mixed.

6. Separate the meat out into 3oz balls, disperse or toss the remnants.

7. Use the 3-in-1 Burger press to create the perfect patty! Place the patties on the grill and cook for 15-20 minutes depending on their thickness. Flip every 5ish minutes.

8. Add the buns to the grill if you'd like them toasted!

9. Remove the turkey sliders (and the buns) from the grill, add spinach, and whatever you think will taste good!

APPETIZERS AND SNACKS

Pigs In A Blanket

Servings: 4-6

Cooking Time: 15 Minutes

Ingredients:

- 2 Tablespoon Poppy Seeds
- 1 Tablespoon Dried Minced Onion
- 2 Teaspoon garlic, minced
- 2 Tablespoon Sesame Seeds
- 1 Teaspoon salt
- 8 Ounce Original Crescent Dough
- 1/4 Cup Dijon mustard
- 1 Large egg, beaten

Directions:

1. When ready to cook, start your smoker at 350 degrees F, and preheat with lid closed, 10 to 15 minutes.

2. Mix together poppy seeds, dried minced onion, dried minced garlic, salt and sesame seeds. Set aside.

3. Cut each triangle of crescent roll dough into thirds lengthwise, making 3 small strips from each roll.

4. Brush the dough strips lightly with Dijon mustard. Put the mini hot dogs on 1 end of the dough and roll up.

5. Arrange them, seam side down, on a greased baking pan. Brush with egg wash and sprinkle with seasoning mixture.

6. Bake in smoker until golden brown, about 12 to 15 minutes.

7. Serve with mustard or dipping sauce of your choice. Enjoy!

Chorizo Queso Fundido

Servings: 4-6   Cooking Time: 20 Minutes

Ingredients:

- 1 poblano chile
- 1 cup chopped queso quesadilla or queso Oaxaca
- 1 cup shredded Monterey Jack cheese
- ¼ cup milk
- 1 tablespoon all-purpose flour
- 2 (4-ounce) links Mexican chorizo sausage, casings removed
- ⅓ cup beer
- 1 tablespoon unsalted butter
- 1 small red onion, chopped
- ½ cup whole kernel corn
- 2 serrano chiles or jalapeño peppers, stemmed, seeded, and coarsely chopped
- 1 tablespoon minced garlic
- 1 tablespoon freshly squeezed lime juice
- 1 teaspoon ground cumin
- 1 teaspoon salt
- 1 teaspoon freshly ground black pepper
- 1 tablespoon chopped fresh cilantro
- 1 tablespoon chopped scallions
- Tortilla chips, for serving

Directions:

1. Supply your smoker with wood pellets and follow the start-up procedure. Preheat, with the lid closed, to 350°F.

2. On the smoker or over medium-high heat on the stove top, place the poblano directly on the grate (or burner) to char for 1 to 2 minutes, turning as needed. Remove from heat and place in a closed-up lunch-size paper bag for 2 minutes to sweat and further loosen the skin.

3. Remove the skin and coarsely chop the poblano, removing the seeds; set aside.

4. In a bowl, combine the queso quesadilla, Monterey Jack, milk, and flour; set aside.

5. On the stove top, in a cast iron skillet over medium heat, cook and crumble the chorizo for about 2 minutes.

6. Transfer the cooked chorizo to a small, grill-safe pan and place over indirect heat on the smoker.

7. Place the cast iron skillet on the preheated grill grate. Pour in the beer and simmer for a few minutes, loosening and stirring in any remaining sausage bits from the pan.

8. Add the butter to the pan, then add the cheese mixture a little at a time, stirring constantly.

9. When the cheese is smooth, stir in the onion, corn, serrano chiles, garlic, lime juice, cuvmin, salt, and pepper. Stir in the reserved chopped charred poblano.

10. Close the lid and smoke for 15 to 20 minutes to infuse the queso with smoke flavor and further cook the vegetables.

11. When the cheese is bubbly, top with the chorizo mixture and garnish with the cilantro and scallions.

12. Serve the chorizo queso fundido hot with tortilla chips.

Bacon Pork Pinwheels (kansas Lollipops)

Servings: 4-6

Cooking Time: 20 Minutes

Ingredients:

➢ 1 Whole Pork Loin, boneless

➢ To Taste salt and pepper

➢ To Taste Greek Seasoning

➢ 4 Slices bacon

➢ To Taste The Ultimate BBQ Sauce

Directions:

1. When ready to cook, start the smoker and set temperature to 500F. Preheat, lid closed, for 10 to 15 minutes.

2. Trim pork loin of any unwanted silver skin or fat. Using a sharp knife, cut pork loin length wise, into 4 long strips.

3. Lay pork flat, then season with salt, pepper and Cavender's Greek Seasoning.

4. Flip the pork strips over and layer bacon on unseasoned side. Begin tightly rolling the pork strips, with bacon being rolled up on the inside.

5. Secure a skewer all the way through each pork roll to secure it in place. Set the pork rolls down on grill and cook for 15 minutes.

6. Brush BBQ Sauce over the pork. Turn each skewer over, then coat the other side. Let pork cook for another 5-10 minutes, depending on thickness of your pork. Enjoy!

Grilled Guacamole

Servings: 6

Cooking Time: 30 Minutes

Ingredients:

- 3 large avocados, halved and pitted
- 1 lime, halved
- ½ jalapeño, deseeded and deveined
- ½ small white or red onion, peeled
- 2 garlic cloves, peeled and skewered on a toothpick
- 1 tsp coarse salt, plus more
- 1½ tbsp reduced-fat mayo
- 2 tbsp chopped fresh cilantro
- 2 tbsp crumbled queso fresco (optional)
- tortilla chips

Directions:

1. Supply your smoker with wood pellets and follow the start-up procedure. Preheat the grill, with the lid closed, to 225° F.

2. Place the avocados, lime, jalapeño, and onion cut sides down on the grate. Use the toothpicks to balance the garlic cloves between the bars. Smoke for 30 minutes. (You want the vegetables to retain most of their rawness.)

3. Transfer everything to a cutting board. Remove the garlic cloves from the toothpick and roughly chop. Sprinkle with the salt and continue to mince the garlic until it begins to form a paste. Scrape the garlic and salt into a large bowl.

4. Scoop the avocado flesh from the peels into the bowl. Squeeze the juice of ½ lime over the avocado. Mash the avocados but leave them somewhat chunky. Finely dice the jalapeño. Dice 2 tablespoons of onion. (Reserve the remaining onion for another use.) Add the jalapeño, onion, mayo, and cilantro to the bowl. Stir gently to combine. Taste for seasoning, adding more salt, lime juice, and jalapeño as desired.

5. Transfer the guacamole to a serving bowl. Top with the queso fresco (if using). Serve with tortilla chips.

Citrus-infused Marinated Olives

Servings: 6

Cooking Time: 30 Minutes

Ingredients:

- 1½ cups mixed brined olives, with pits
- ½ cup extra virgin olive oil
- 1 tbsp freshly squeezed lemon juice
- 1 garlic clove, peeled and thinly sliced
- 1 tsp smoked Spanish paprika
- 2 sprigs of fresh rosemary
- 2 sprigs of fresh thyme
- 2 bay leaves, fresh or dried
- 1 small dried red chili pepper, deseeded and flesh crumbled, or ¼ tsp crushed red pepper flakes
- 3 strips of orange zest
- 3 strips of lemon zest

Directions:

1. Supply your smoker with wood pellets and follow the start-up procedure. Preheat the grill, with the lid closed, to 180° F.

2. Drain the olives, reserving 1 tablespoon of brine. Spread the olives in a single layer in an aluminum foil roasting pan. Place the pan on the grate and cook the olives for 30 minutes, stirring the olives or shaking the pan once or twice.

3. In a small saucepan on the stovetop over low heat, warm the olive oil. Whisk in the lemon juice and the reserved 1 tablespoon of brine. Stir in the garlic and paprika. Add the rosemary, thyme, bay leaves, chili pepper, and orange and lemon zests. Warm over low heat for 10 minutes. Remove the saucepan from the heat.

4. Transfer the olives and olive oil mixture to a pint jar. Tuck the aromatics around the sides of the jar. Let cool and then cover and refrigerate for up to 5 days. Let the olives come to room temperature before serving.

Bacon-wrapped Jalapeño Poppers

Servings: 12

Cooking Time: 30 Minutes

Ingredients:

- 8 ounces cream cheese, softened
- ½ cup shredded Cheddar cheese
- ¼ cup chopped scallions
- 1 teaspoon chipotle chile powder or regular chili powder
- 1 teaspoon garlic powder
- 1 teaspoon salt
- 18 large jalapeño peppers, stemmed, seeded, and halved lengthwise
- 1 pound bacon (precooked works well)

Directions:

1. Supply your smoker with wood pellets and follow the start-up procedure. Preheat, with the lid closed, to 350°F. Line a baking sheet with aluminum foil.

2. In a small bowl, combine the cream cheese, Cheddar cheese, scallions, chipotle powder, garlic powder, and salt.

3. Stuff the jalapeño halves with the cheese mixture.

4. Cut the bacon into pieces big enough to wrap around the stuffed pepper halves.

5. Wrap the bacon around the peppers and place on the prepared baking sheet.

6. Put the baking sheet on the grill grate, close the lid, and smoke the peppers for 30 minutes, or until the cheese is melted and the bacon is cooked through and crisp.

7. Let the jalapeño poppers cool for 3 to 5 minutes. Serve warm.

Sriracha & Maple Cashews

Servings: 10

Cooking Time: 60 Minutes

Ingredients:

- 2 tbsp unsalted butter
- 3 tbsp pure maple syrup
- 1 tbsp sriracha
- 1 tsp coarse salt (use only if nuts are unsalted)
- 2½ cups unsalted cashews

Directions:

1. Supply your smoker with wood pellets and follow the start-up procedure. Preheat the grill, with the lid closed, to 250° F.

2. In a small saucepan on the stovetop over low heat, melt the butter. Add the maple syrup, sriracha, and salt (if using). Stir until combined. Add the nuts and stir gently to coat thoroughly.

3. Spread the nuts in a single layer in an aluminum foil roasting pan coated with cooking spray. Place the pan on the grate and smoke the nuts until they're lightly toasted, about 1 hour, stirring once or twice.

4. Remove the pan from the grill and let the nuts cool for 15 minutes. They'll be sticky at first but will crisp up. Break them up with your fingers and store at room temperature in an airtight container, such as a lidded glass jar.

Pig Pops (sweet-hot Bacon On A Stick)

Servings: 24

Cooking Time: 30 Minutes

Ingredients:

- ➢ Nonstick cooking spray, oil, or butter, for greasing
- ➢ 2 pounds thick-cut bacon (24 slices)
- ➢ 24 metal skewers
- ➢ 1 cup packed light brown sugar
- ➢ 2 to 3 teaspoons cayenne pepper
- ➢ ½ cup maple syrup, divided

Directions:

1. Supply your smoker with wood pellets and follow the start-up procedure. Preheat, with the lid closed, to 350°F.

2. Coat a disposable aluminum foil baking sheet with cooking spray, oil, or butter.

3. Thread each bacon slice onto a metal skewer and place on the prepared baking sheet.

4. In a medium bowl, stir together the brown sugar and cayenne.

5. Baste the top sides of the bacon with ¼ cup of maple syrup.

6. Sprinkle half of the brown sugar mixture over the bacon.

7. Place the baking sheet on the grill, close the lid, and smoke for 15 to 30 minutes.

8. Using tongs, flip the bacon skewers. Baste with the remaining ¼ cup of maple syrup and top with the remaining brown sugar mixture.

9. Continue smoking with the lid closed for 10 to 15 minutes, or until crispy. You can eyeball the bacon and smoke to your desired doneness, but the actual ideal internal temperature for bacon is 155°F

10. Using tongs, carefully remove the bacon skewers from the grill. Let cool completely before handling.

Smoked Turkey Sandwich

Servings: 1

Cooking Time: 15 Minutes

Ingredients:

- ➢ 2 slices sourdough bread
- ➢ 2 tablespoons butter, at room temperature
- ➢ 2 (1-ounce) slices Swiss cheese
- ➢ 4 ounces leftover Smoked Turkey
- ➢ 1 teaspoon garlic salt

Directions:

1. Supply your smoker with wood pellets and follow the start-up procedure. Preheat the grill, with the lid closed, to 375°F.

2. Coat one side of each bread slice with 1 tablespoon of butter and sprinkle the buttered sides with garlic salt.

3. Place 1 slice of cheese on each unbuttered side of the bread, and then put the turkey on the cheese.

4. Close the sandwich, buttered sides out, and place it directly on the grill grate. Cook for 5 minutes. Flip the sandwich and cook for 5 minutes more. Remove the sandwich from the grill, cut it in half, and serve.

Bayou Wings With Cajun Rémoulade

Ingredients:

- 16 large whole chicken wings or 32 drumettes and flats, about 3lb (1.4kg) total
- for the rub
- 1 tbsp kosher salt
- 1 tsp freshly ground black pepper
- 1 tsp paprika
- ½ tsp ground cayenne, plus more
- ½ tsp garlic powder
- ½ tsp celery salt
- ½ tsp dried thyme
- 2 tbsp vegetable oil
- for the rémoulade
- 1¼ cups reduced-fat mayo
- ¼ cup Creole-style or whole grain mustard
- 2 tbsp horseradish
- 2 tbsp pickle relish
- 1 tbsp freshly squeezed lemon juice
- 1 tsp paprika, plus more
- 1 tsp hot sauce, plus more
- 1 tsp Worcestershire sauce
- coarse salt
- for serving
- lemon wedges
- pickled okra (optional)

Directions:

1. Supply your smoker with wood pellets and follow the start-up procedure. Preheat the grill, with the lid closed, to 350° F.

2. If using whole wings, cut through the two joints, separating them into drumettes, flats, and wing tips. (Discard the wing tips or save them for chicken stock.) Alternatively, leave the wings whole. Place the chicken in a resealable plastic bag.

3. In a small bowl, make the rub by combining the ingredients. Mix well. Pour the rub over the wings and toss them to thoroughly coat. Refrigerate for 2 hours.

4. In a small bowl, make the Cajun rémoulade by whisking together the mayo, mustard, horseradish, pickle relish, lemon juice, paprika, hot sauce, and Worcestershire. Season with salt to taste. The mixture should be highly seasoned. Transfer to a serving bowl and lightly dust with paprika. Cover and refrigerate until ready to serve.

5. Remove the wings from the refrigerator and allow the excess marinade to drip off. Place the wings on the grate at an angle to the bars. Grill for 20 minutes and then turn. (They'll brown more evenly but will also have less of a tendency to stick.) Continue to cook until the wings are nicely browned and the meat is no longer pink at the bone, about 20 minutes more.

6. Remove the wings from the grill and pile them on a platter. Serve with the Cajun rémoulade, lemon wedges, and pickled okra (if using).

Chuckwagon Beef Jerky

Servings: 6   Cooking Time: 300 Minutes

Ingredients:

- 2½lb (1.2kg) boneless top or bottom round steak, sirloin tip, flank steak, or venison
- 1 cup sugar-free dark-colored soda
- 1 cup cold brewed coffee
- ½ cup light soy sauce
- ¼ cup Worcestershire sauce

- 2 tbsp whiskey (optional)
- 2 tsp chili powder
- 1½ tsp garlic salt
- 1 tsp onion powder
- 1 tsp pink curing salt

Directions:

1. Slice the meat into ¼-inch-thick (.5cm) strips, trimming off any visible fat or gristle. (Slice against the grain for more tender jerky and with the grain for chewier jerky.) Place the meat in a large resealable plastic bag.

2. In a small bowl, whisk together the soda, coffee, soy sauce, Worcestershire sauce, whiskey (if using), chili powder, garlic salt, onion powder, and curing salt (if using). Whisk until the salt dissolves. Pour the mixture over the meat and reseal the bag. Refrigerate for 24 to 48 hours, turning the bag several times to redistribute the brine.

3. Supply your smoker with wood pellets and follow the start-up procedure. Preheat the grill, with the lid closed, to 150° F.

4. Drain the meat and discard the brine. Place the strips of meat in a single layer on paper towels and blot any excess moisture.

5. Place the meat in a single layer on the grate and smoke for 4 to 5 hours, turning once or twice. (If you're aware of hot spots on your grate, rotate the strips so they smoke evenly.) To test for doneness, bend one or two pieces in the middle. They should be dry but still somewhat pliant. Or simply eat a piece to see if it's done to your liking.

6. For the best texture, when you remove the meat from the grill, place the still-warm jerky in a resealable plastic bag and let rest for 30 minutes. (You might see condensation form on the inside of the bag, but the moisture will be reabsorbed by the meat.) Or let the meat cool completely and then store in a resealable plastic bag or covered container. The jerky will last a few days at room temperature but will last longer (up to 2 weeks) if refrigerated.

Delicious Deviled Crab Appetizer

Servings: 30

Cooking Time: 10 Minutes

Ingredients:

- Nonstick cooking spray, oil, or butter, for greasing
- 1 cup panko breadcrumbs, divided
- 1 cup canned corn, drained
- ½ cup chopped scallions, divided
- ½ red bell pepper, finely chopped
- 16 ounces jumbo lump crabmeat
- ¾ cup mayonnaise, divided
- 1 egg, beaten
- 1 teaspoon salt
- 1 teaspoon freshly ground black pepper
- 2 teaspoons cayenne pepper, divided
- Juice of 1 lemon

Directions:

1. Supply your smoker with wood pellets and follow the start-up procedure. Preheat, with the lid closed, to 425°F.

2. Spray three 12-cup mini muffin pans with cooking spray and divide ½ cup of the panko between 30 of the muffin cups, pressing into the bottoms and up the sides. (Work in batches, if necessary, depending on the number of pans you have.)

3. In a medium bowl, combine the corn, ¼ cup of scallions, the bell pepper, crabmeat, half of the mayonnaise, the egg, salt, pepper, and 1 teaspoon of cayenne pepper.

4. Gently fold in the remaining ½ cup of breadcrumbs and divide the mixture between the prepared mini muffin cups.

5. Place the pans on the grill grate, close the lid, and smoke for 10 minutes, or until golden brown.

6. In a small bowl, combine the lemon juice and the remaining mayonnaise, scallions, and cayenne pepper to make a sauce.

7. Brush the tops of the mini crab cakes with the sauce and serve hot.

BEEF LAMB AND GAME RECIPES

Lime Carne Asada Tacos

Servings: 4

Cooking Time: 10 Minutes

Ingredients:

- 1/2 Tsp Black Pepper
- 1 Tsp Garlic Powder
- 2 Lime, Juiced
- 1 Tsp Salt
- 1 1/2 Lbs Steak, Skirt
- 8 Tortilla

Directions:

1. Supply your smoker with wood pellets and follow the start-up procedure. Preheat the grill, with the lid closed, to 400° F. Place the steaks on the grill, and grill them for 4-8 minutes, then flip the steaks and grill for an additional 4-8 minutes.

2. Remove steaks from the grill, loosely cover them with foil, and let them sit for 5-10 minutes. Next chop the steaks into pieces and serve with tortillas and any desired toppings.

Grilled Lemon Skirt Steak

Servings: 1-2

Cooking Time: 5 Minutes

Ingredients:

- ➤ 2 Cloves Garlic, Chopped
- ➤ 1 Lemon, Juice
- ➤ 2 Tablespoons Mustard, Grainy
- ➤ 1/4 Cup Olive Oil
- ➤ 2 Tablespoons Java Chophouse Seasoning
- ➤ 2 Pounds Skirt Steak, Trimmed
- ➤ 1 Tablespoon Worcestershire Sauce

Directions:

1. In a small bowl, mix together the   Java Chophouse Seasoning, oil, garlic, lemon juice, and Worcestershire. Generously rub the mixture all over the skirt steak and allow to marinate for 45 minutes.

2. Supply your smoker with wood pellets and follow the start-up procedure. Preheat the grill, with the lid closed, to 400° F.

3. Grill the skirt steaks for 3-5 minutes on each side or until the steak is done to the desired degree of doneness.

4. Remove the steaks from the grill and allow to rest for 5 minutes before slicing and serving.

Blackened Saskatchewan Tomahawk Steaks

Servings: 4

Cooking Time: 45 Minutes

Ingredients:

- 2 Whole tomahawk steaks
- 4 Tablespoon Blackened Saskatchewan Rub
- 2 Tablespoon butter

Directions:

1. Supply your smoker with wood pellets and follow the start-up procedure. Preheat the grill, with the lid closed, to 225° F.

2. Cover cold steaks in the Blackened Saskatchewan Rub. Let rest 10 minutes for the seasoning to adhere.

3. Place steaks directly on grill grates and smoke for about 40 minutes, or until an internal temp reaches 119°F. Remove from grill and wrap tightly in foil to rest.

4. Turn up temperature on the grill to 400°F - with a cast iron pan or griddle inside. When the pan is hot, add 2 Tbsp of butter and sear the first steak, about 2-4 minutes per side, or until the internal temperature reads 125°F - 130°F. Repeat with the other Tomahawk. Rest, slice, serve. Enjoy!

Chocolate Bark Brisket

Servings: 8

Cooking Time: 720 Minutes

Ingredients:

- ➢ 1 Whole Beef Brisket, Fat Trimmed to 1/4" Thickness
- ➢ 1/3 Cup Jacobsen Salt Co. Pure Kosher Sea Salt
- ➢ 2 Tablespoon garlic powder
- ➢ 2 Tablespoon onion powder
- ➢ 1/3 Cup freshly ground black pepper

Directions:

1. Chef Tip: Ask for a brisket that is as evenly thick as possible, with the surrounding fat trimmed to 1/4" thick, this protects the meat from drying out while cooking. You will want to make plans to special order your brisket ahead of time (the brisket already sold at the meat counter is typically not whole).

2. Season the meat the day before. Mix salt, garlic, onion powder, and pepper in a small bowl and season the meat all over.

3. Supply your smoker with wood pellets and follow the start-up procedure. Preheat the grill, with the lid closed, to 250° F. Place brisket, fatty side up, on grill grate right in the middle. Chef Tip: Resist the urge to open the grill often, this will cause the temperature to fluctuate. Check pellets every 45 minutes or so. We recommend using a stand-alone thermometer to ensure an accurate reading. Stick it through the gap between the lid and base of the grill. When the brisket reaches an internal temperature of 160-165° degrees F, start to rotate the brisket every 3 hours and flip as needed if top or bottom is coloring faster than the other. Grill: 225 °F Probe: 165 °F

4. Chef Tip: Wrap brisket in foil until meat reaches an internal temperature of 203° degrees F. What's important is getting a smoky flavor into the meat, and 5-6 hours on the grill should do it. After that point, you're simply getting the meat cooked through. Grill: 225 °F Probe: 203 °F

5. When the brisket reaches an internal temperature of 203° degrees F, it's done. Let the brisket rest for one hour. You will want to plastic wrap it and then wrap it in foil for this period of time. Slice and serve. Enjoy!

Venison Carne Asada

Servings: 4   Cooking Time: 8 Minutes

Ingredients:

- 1½lb (680g) venison steak, such as sirloin, about ¾ inch (2cm) thick
- southwestern-style rub
- 12 large scallions or spring onions, cleaned and trimmed
- for the marinade
- 2 garlic cloves, peeled and smashed with a chef's knife
- 1 jalapeño or serrano pepper, destemmed and thinly sliced
- juice of 1 orange
- juice of 1 lime
- 1 tbsp distilled white vinegar
- 1 tsp ground cumin
- 1 tsp coarse salt
- ⅓ cup vegetable oil
- ¼ cup chopped fresh cilantro
- for serving
- warmed flour or corn tortillas (optional)
- lime wedges
- sprigs of fresh cilantro
- Salsa de Molcajete or another salsa

Directions:

1. In a small bowl, make the marinade by combining the garlic, jalapeño, orange juice, lime juice, white vinegar, cumin, and salt. Whisk until the salt dissolves. Whisk in the vegetable oil and stir in the cilantro. Place the venison in a resealable plastic bag and add the marinade, massaging the bag to thoroughly coat the meat. Refrigerate for 2 to 4 hours.

2. Supply your smoker with wood pellets and follow the start-up procedure. Preheat the grill, with the lid closed, to 450° F.

3. Drain the venison and remove any solids. (Discard the marinade.) Pat dry with paper towels. Lightly dust on both sides with the rub. Place the venison and scallions on the grate and sear until the internal temperature reaches 135°F (57°C), about 3 to 4 minutes per side. Grill the scallions until the bulbs are browned and tender, about 4 to 6 minutes, turning as needed.

4. Remove the meat and scallions from the grill. Place the venison on a cutting board and let rest for 3 minutes. Slice thinly on a sharp diagonal. Shingle the meat on a platter. Scatter the scallions and cilantro over the top. Serve with tortillas (if using), lime wedges, cilantro, and salsa.

Crusted Prime Rib With Rosemary

Servings: 4-6

Cooking Time: 180 Minutes

Ingredients:

- ➢ 4-6 garlic, cloves
- ➢ 1/3 cup olive oil
- ➢ chop house steak seasoning
- ➢ 7 pound, boned tied and rolled prime rib roast
- ➢ 3 tablespoon rosemary, fresh
- ➢ 3 tablespoon thyme, fresh sprigs

Directions:

1. In a food processor, blend together the garlic, rosemary, thyme, sage, and oil until a rough paste forms. Place the prime rib on a sheet pan over a wire rack and rub the prime rib generously with the herb paste on all sides.

2. Season the prime rib with   Chop House Steak Seasoning generously on all sides, then chill uncovered in the refrigerator overnight, or for 12 hours.

3. Once the prime rib has chilled for 12 hours, supply your smoker with wood pellets and follow the start-up procedure. Preheat the grill, with the lid closed, to 250° F, and grill for 2 hours or until the internal temperature of the roast reaches 110°F, then increase the temperature to 400 and grill for an additional 15-30 minutes, or until the internal temperature reaches 125 - 140°F.

4. Remove the prime rib from the grill, cover tightly in foil and allow to rest for 30 minutes. The final temperature of the prime rib should be 125 - 140°F after resting. Serve and enjoy!

Delicious Grilled Steak

Servings: 2-4

Cooking Time: 25 Minutes

Ingredients:

➤ Steak Seasoning

➤ 2 (1 1/4 Thick) Steak, Bone-In Ribeye

Directions:

1. Make some perfectly grilled steaks and add some Chop House Steak Rub seasoning too!

2. No more than an hour before grilling, let steaks come to room temperature.

3. Generously sprinkle Chop House Steak Rub to both sides of each steak, allowing time for the rub to melt into the meat.

4. Supply your smoker with wood pellets and follow the start-up procedure. Preheat the grill, with the lid closed, to 400° F.

5. Once the grill reaches temperature, Place steaks directly on the grill. For a medium done steak, sear each side for 5-7 minutes, flipping the steaks only one. Adjust time to your desired doneness.

6. Remove steaks from the grill, cover with tin foil, and let it sit 10 minutes before slicing and serving.

Note: Use tongs to flip steaks. Do not flip steaks with a fork or cut into the meat until ready to serve. Any cuts or punctures in the meat will cause juices to escape and dry out your steak.

Smoked Corned Beef Brisket

Servings: 4

Cooking Time: 300 Minutes

Ingredients:

- 1 (3 lb) flat cut corned beef brisket, fat cap at least 1/4 inch thick
- 1 Bottle Apricot BBQ Sauce
- 1/4 Cup Dijon mustard

Directions:

1. Remove the corned beef brisket from its packaging and discard the spice packet, if any. Soak the corned beef in water for at least 8 hours changing the water every 2 hours.

2. Supply your smoker with wood pellets and follow the start-up procedure. Preheat the grill, with the lid closed, to 275° F.

3. Put the brisket directly on the grill grate, fat side up and cook for 2 hours. Grill: 275 °F

4. Meanwhile, combine the Traeger Apricot BBQ Sauce and the Dijon mustard in a medium bowl, whisking to mix.

5. Pour half of the BBQ sauce-mustard mixture in the bottom of a disposable aluminum foil pan. With tongs, transfer the brisket to the pan, fat-side up. Pour the remainder of the BBQ sauce-mustard mixture over the top of the brisket, using a spatula to spread the sauce evenly. Cover the pan tightly with aluminum foil.

6. Return the brisket to the grill and continue to cook for 2 to 3 hours, or until the brisket is tender. The internal temperature should be 203°F on an instant-read meat thermometer. Probe: 203 °F

7. Remove from the grill and allow the meat to rest for 15 to 20 minutes at room temperature. Slice across the grain into 1/4 inch slices with a sharp knife and serve immediately. Enjoy!

Bbq Burnt Ends

Servings: 6

Cooking Time: 540 Minutes

Ingredients:

- 1 (4-6 lb) point cut brisket
- 2 Cup beef broth
- 12 Ounce Texas Spicy BBQ Sauce
- Beef Rub

Directions:

1. Supply your smoker with wood pellets and follow the start-up procedure. Preheat the grill, with the lid closed, to 250° F.

2. Combine broth and sauce in small bowl and set aside. Trim excess fat off brisket point and rub brisket with Traeger Beef Rub.

3. Place brisket on the grill grate and cook until the internal temperature reaches 190℉ (approximately 6 to 7 hours). Remove brisket from grill and cut into 1 inch cubes. Grill: 250 ℉ Probe: 190 ℉

4. Toss brisket cubes with sauce mixture in a pan and cover the pan with aluminum foil. Place pan in grill and cook for 1 hour. Grill: 250 ℉

5. Stir the burnt ends and cook for an additional hour. Enjoy!

Georgia Smoked Onion Brisket Sandwich

Servings: 4

Cooking Time: 450 Minutes

Ingredients:

- ½ Cup Barbecue Sauce
- ¼ Cup Beef Broth
- 2 Tablespoons Bourbon
- 1, 3 Pound Brisket Flat, Trimmed
- 4 Kaiser Rolls
- ½ Cup Peach Preserves
- Sliced Pickles
- 4 Tablespoons Pulled Pork Rub
- Sliced White Onions

Directions:

1. Supply your smoker with wood pellets and follow the start-up procedure. Preheat the grill, with the lid closed, to 225° F.

2. Generously rub the brisket with the Pulled Pork Rub. Set aside.

3. In a bowl, mix together the barbecue sauce, peach preserves and bourbon. Set aside.

4. Place the brisket in the smoker and smoke for 5 hours, or until the internal temperature reaches 170°F. Once the brisket reaches temperature, remove from the smoker, place the brisket in foil and pour the beef broth over the top. Wrap the brisket tightly in aluminum foil and return to the smoker for another 2 hours, or until the internal temperature reaches 190°F.

5. Remove the brisket from the grill, unwrap the brisket, discard the foil, and brush the brisket generously with the peach glaze mixture. Place the brisket back on the smoker and smoke for 30 minutes, or until the brisket is shiny and glazed. Remove the brisket from the grill and rest for 10 minutes, covered in foil.

6. Once the brisket has rested, slice thickly against the grain and top the Kaiser rolls with the brisket slices, onion slices and pickle slices. Serve immediately.

Reverse-seared Tri-tip

Servings: 4

Cooking Time: 180 Minutes

Ingredients:

➢ 1½ pounds tri-tip roast

➢ 1 batch Espresso Brisket Rub

Directions:

1. Supply your smoker with wood pellets and follow the start-up procedure. Preheat the grill, with the lid closed, to 180°F.

2. Season the tri-tip roast with the rub. Using your hands, work the rub into the meat.

3. Place the roast directly on the grill grate and smoke until its internal temperature reaches 140°F.

4. Increase the grill's temperature to 450°F and continue to cook until the roast's internal temperature reaches 145°F. This same technique can be done over an open flame or in a cast-iron skillet with some butter.

5. Remove the tri-tip roast from the grill and let it rest 10 to 15 minutes, before slicing and serving.

Cheesy Nachos

Servings: 8

Cooking Time: 20 Minutes

Ingredients:

- Cilantro
- Olive Oil
- Pepper
- 1 Red Bell Peppers, Sliced
- 2 Rib-Eye Steaks
- Salsa
- Salt
- 1 Cup Shredded Cheddar Cheese
- Sour Cream
- 1 Yellow Bell Pepper, Sliced
- 1 Zucchini, Sliced

Directions:

1. Supply your smoker with wood pellets and follow the start-up procedure. Preheat the grill, with the lid closed, to 400° F.

2. Coat both sides of the steak with olive oil and season with sea salt and pepper. Place the steak on the grates and grill for about 4 to 5 minutes per side.

3. Remove the steak off the grill and let rest for about 10 minutes before cutting into bite-sized strips.

4. Brush with barbecue sauce if desired.

5. Empty a large bag of nacho chips evenly into a cast iron pan. Start loading up with toppings - steak, cheddar cheese, sautéed vegetables.

6. These are just suggested toppings, so feel free to add anything you like!

7. Place your loaded nachos on the grill and let the hot smoke melt your toppings into one hearty creation.

8. Cook for about 10 minutes, or until the cheese has fully melted.

9. Remove and serve with sour cream and salsa.

COCKTAILS RECIPES

Grilled Hawaiian Sour

Servings: 2

Cooking Time: 15 Minutes

Ingredients:

- 2 Whole pineapple, trimmed and sliced
- 1/2 Cup palm sugar
- 3 Ounce bourbon
- 2 Ounce grilled pineapple juice
- 2 Ounce Smoked Simple Syrup
- 10 Ounce lemon juice
- 2 grilled pineapple chunk, for garnish
- 2 pineapple leaf, for garnish

Directions:

1. Supply your smoker with wood pellets and follow the start-up procedure. Preheat the grill, with the lid closed, to 350° F.

2. For the Grilled Pineapple Juice: Dust pineapple slices with palm sugar. Place directly on the grill grate and cook for 8 minutes per side. Grill: 350 ℉

3. Remove from grill and let cool. Reserve a few pieces for garnish. Run remaining pineapple pieces through centrifugal juicer to extract juice.

4. To Make the Drink: Add bourbon, grilled pineapple juice, simple syrup and lemon juice to a cocktail strainer with ice. Shake vigorously. Double strain into a chilled coupe glass. Garnish with grilled pineapple chunk and pineapple leaf. Enjoy!

Grilled Peach Smash Cocktail

Servings: 2

Cooking Time: 10 Minutes

Ingredients:

- 2 peach, sliced and grilled
- 10 fresh mint leaves
- 1 1/2 Ounce Smoked Simple Syrup
- 4 Ounce bourbon
- 2 mint sprig, for garnish

Directions:

1. Supply your smoker with wood pellets and follow the start-up procedure. Preheat the grill, with the lid closed, to 375° F.

2. Cut the peach into 6 slices and brush with Traeger Smoked Simple Syrup. Place directly on the grill grate and cook 10 to 12 minutes or until peaches soften and get grill marks. Grill: 375 ℉

3. In a mixing glass, add 3 slices of grilled peaches, 5 mint leaves and Traeger Smoked Simple Syrup.

4. Muddle ingredients to release oils of the mint and juices from the grilled peaches. Add bourbon and crushed ice.

5. Shake and pour into a stemless wine glass. Top off with more crushed ice. Garnish with a grilled peach and mint sprig. Enjoy!

Smoked Salted Caramel White Russian

Servings: 4

Cooking Time: 20 Minutes

Ingredients:

➢ 16 Ounce half-and-half

➢ salted caramel sauce

➢ 6 Ounce vodka

➢ 6 Ounce Kahlúa

Directions:

1. Supply your smoker with wood pellets and follow the start-up procedure. Preheat the grill, with the lid closed, to 180° F.

2. Pour the half-and-half in a shallow baking dish and place directly on the grill grate. In another shallow baking dish, pour 2 to 3 cups of water and place on the grill next to the half-and-half.

3. Smoke both the half-and-half and water for 20 minutes. Remove from the grill and let cool. Grill: 180 ˚F

4. Place the half-and-half in the fridge until ready to use. Pour the smoked water into ice cube trays and transfer to the freezer until completely frozen.

5. Separate the smoked ice cubes into four glasses. Drizzle the salted caramel sauce around the inside of the glass.

6. Pour 1-1/2 ounce vodka and 1-1/2 ounce Kahlúa into each of the glasses and top with the smoked half-and-half. Enjoy!

Smoked Jacobsen Salt Margarita

Servings: 2

Cooking Time: 1 Day

Ingredients:

- kosher sea salt
- 3 Cup Jacobsen Co. Honey
- 6 Ounce tequila
- 4 Ounce fresh squeezed lime juice
- 1/2 Cup Jacobsen Salt Co. Cherrywood Smoked Salt or smoked kosher salt
- 2 Ounce simple syrup
- 2 Teaspoon orange liqueur

Directions:

1. If making your own smoked salt, take kosher sea salt (however much you want to smoke) and spread it out on a tray.

2. Supply your smoker with wood pellets and follow the start-up procedure. Preheat the grill, with the lid closed, to 165° F.

3. Place tray of salt directly on the grill grate and smoke for about 24 hours, stirring the salt every 8 hours. Once it has smoked for 24 hours, take off grill and use in all your favorite dishes. Note: If you want to skip the long smoke session, use Jacobsen Salt Co. Cherrywood Smoked Salt. Grill: 165 ˚F

4. Simple Syrup: Put the honey and 1 cup water in a small saucepan. Cook over low heat, stirring, for about 20 min.

5. Fill a cocktail shaker with ice. Add tequila, lime juice, simple syrup and orange liqueur. Cover and shake until mixed and chilled, about 30 seconds.

6. Place smoked salt on a plate. Press the rim of a chilled rocks glass into the salt to rim the edge. Strain margarita into the glass. Enjoy!

Smoking Gun Cocktail

Servings: 2

Cooking Time: 45 Minutes

Ingredients:

- ➢ 2 Jar vermouth soaked cocktail onions
- ➢ 3 Ounce vodka
- ➢ 1 Ounce dry vermouth

Directions:

1. Supply your smoker with wood pellets and follow the start-up procedure. Preheat the grill, with the lid closed, to 180° F.

2. To make the smoked onion vermouth: Pour jar of vermouth soaked cocktail onions onto a shallow sheet pan. Smoke for 45 minutes. Remove from grill and set aside to chill. Grill: 180 ℉

3. To make the cocktail: Add vodka, 1 teaspoon liquid from the smoked onions and dry vermouth to a mixing glass. Shake and strain into a chilled martini glass.

4. Garnish with smoked cocktail onions on a skewer. Enjoy!

A Smoking Classic Cocktail

Servings: 2

Cooking Time: 60 Minutes

Ingredients:

- 2 Bottle Angostura orange bitters
- 10 sugar cubes
- 8 Ounce Champagne
- lemon twist

Directions:

1. Supply your smoker with wood pellets and follow the start-up procedure. Preheat the grill, with the lid closed, to 180° F.

2. For the Smoked Orange Bitters: In a small skillet, combine 1 bottle of Angostura orange bitters with a splash of water and 4 sugar cubes.

3. Place skillet on the grill grate and smoke for 60 minutes. Cool the smoked bitters and put back into the bottle. Grill: 180 ˚F

4. Add a sugar cube to each Champagne flute and soak the sugar cubes with the smoked bitters.

5. Add champagne and a lemon twist in a flute glass. Enjoy!

Smoked Hibiscus Sparkler

Servings: 4

Cooking Time: 30 Minutes

Ingredients:

- 1/2 Cup sugar
- 2 Tablespoon dried hibiscus flowers
- 1 Bottle sparkling wine
- crystallized ginger, for garnish

Directions:

1. Supply your smoker with wood pellets and follow the start-up procedure. Preheat the grill, with the lid closed, to 180° F.

2. Place water in a shallow baking dish and place directly on the grill grate. Smoke the water for 30 minutes or until desired smoke flavor is achieved. Grill: 180 °F

3. Pour water into a small saucepan and add sugar and hibiscus flowers. Bring to a simmer over medium heat and cook until sugar is dissolved.

4. Strain out the hibiscus flowers and transfer your simple syrup to a small container and refrigerate until chilled.

5. Pour 1/2 ounce smoked hibiscus simple syrup in the bottom of a champagne glass and top with sparkling wine.

6. Drop in a few pieces of crystallized ginger to garnish. Enjoy!

Dublin Delight Cocktail

Servings: 2

Cooking Time: 20 Minutes

Ingredients:

- 2 orange, sliced
- 3 Fluid Ounce Teeling Whiskey
- 1 1/2 Fluid Ounce Smoked Simple Syrup
- 6 Dash aromatic bitters
- 6 Fluid Ounce Guinness beer
- 2 Amarena cherry, for garnish

Directions:

1. Supply your smoker with wood pellets and follow the start-up procedure. Preheat the grill, with the lid closed, to 450° F.

2. Place orange slices directly on the grill grate and cook 20 to 25 minutes. Remove from grill and let cool. Grill: 450 °F

3. In a mixing glass, add whiskey, Traeger Smoked Simple Syrup and bitters. Add ice and shake. Pour over a beer glass filled with ice and top off with cold Guinness.

4. Garnish with a grilled orange slice and Amarena cherry. Enjoy!

9 781803 202112